BEYOND THE WILD BUNCH

THE FAST-GROWING SPORT OF COWBOY ACTION SHOOTING

The author wishes to acknowledge the editorial contributions of
Mike Dillon, Barrett Tillman, Mark Pixler, and picture layout by Wynter Copeland;
Dillon Precision Products, Inc., for contributions from its photograph collection;
The Single Action Shooting Society (SASS) for Appendix A; and
The Cowboy Mounted Shooting Association (CMSA) for Appendix B.

END of TRAIL®, SASS®, Single Action Shooting Society®, Cowboy Action Shooting™ (CAS), The World Championship of Cowboy Action Shooting™,
The Cowboy Chronicle™, bow-legged cowboy design, and the rocking horse design are all trademarks of The Single Action Shooting Society®, Inc.

Cover Photo Credits:
Gary Bartholomew, aka Sassquatch; Tim Coker, aka Justice B. Dunn; Al Nordeen, aka Būho Grande; Jim Price, aka Jim Blade.
Special thanks to Craig Nelson, "The Wild Bunch" set fabricator; Bryce Hatfield and Ray Trujillo, ACME Cruise Missile Division;
Joe Swanson, purveyor of blank ammunition; and Mike Smith, Dillon Staff Photographer.

Thanks to Michael J. Klein of Hollywood Cowboy, A Gallery of Vintage Western Movie Posters,
P.O. Box 8142, Scottsdale, AZ 85252-8142, www.hollywoodcowboy.com.

Thanks to the folks at *American Handgunner* Magazine for their generosity
in allowing us to use Nyle Leatham's photographs.

For information, contact:
Dillon Precision Products, Inc.
8009 E. Dillon's Way
Scottsdale, AZ 85260
(800) 223-4570

ISBN 0-9673987-0-3
Printed in Korea

BEYOND THE WILD BUNCH
THE FAST-GROWING SPORT OF COWBOY ACTION SHOOTING

BY GARY KIEFT

PHOTOS BY NYLE LEATHAM
(OR FROM THE DILLON PRECISION PRODUCTS, INC. COLLECTION)

PUBLISHED BY DILLON PRECISION PRODUCTS, INC.,

MICHAEL J. DILLON, PUBLISHER

This book is dedicated to Roy Rogers, King of the Cowboys, who for so many of us personified "the spirit of the game" and to Robert "Howdy Stranger" Palumbo, my late, great pard.

Gary Kieft

JOCK MAHONEY
THE RANGE RIDER

I confess. I started shooting because I was playing cowboy. My first centerfire handgun was an early model Colt Single Action with a 4-3/4" barrel. I bought it from my neighbor for 50 bucks. My first centerfire rifle was a Model 94 Winchester. Yes, it was the TV cowboys that got me started, and The Range Rider was my favorite. He wore his gun belt over a long buckskin shirt with long fringe on the sleeves. I wanted to look just like him. Years later, I got a hand-me-down buckskin shirt. It felt wet and clammy and looked like a shapeless bag on me. So much for boyhood dreams.

Mike Dillon, President
Dillon Precision Products, Inc.

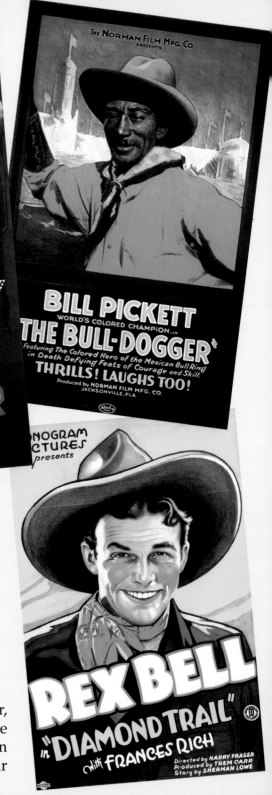

> # "A fiery horse
> with the speed of light,
> a cloud of dust,
> and a hearty 'Hi-Yo Silver!'
> The Lone Ranger rides again!
>
> *Return with us now to those
> thrilling days of yesteryear..."*

That was the invitation of The Lone Ranger's narrator, and that's the invitation we extend to you now as we take you into the exciting world of Cowboy Action Shooting. A world in which adults can fulfill their most cherished childhood fantasies.

TABLE OF CONTENTS

INTRODUCTION

A shooter stands in the shadows of a doorway. He is waiting for a hint that something is about to cut loose. Suddenly, a sound gets his attention. He steps out, raises his Colt, and fires at five oncoming "desperadoes." Then he quickly moves to his horse, pulls a mule-eared shotgun from a scabbard, loads it, and knocks down two more "hardcases." Adrenaline pumping, he breaks open the shotgun, shakes out the empties and crams in two more rounds; yanking the hammers back simultaneously, he pivots and fires again, knocking over another pair of "baddies."

No, this is not a scene from a Louis L'amour novel. This is a look at one of the fastest-growing shooting sports in the world. Cowboy Action Shooting uses metal reactive targets, electronic timers and presents shooting problems in a scenario for the individual to solve. Unlike other shooting sports, Cowboy Action Shooting calls for the use of single-action revolvers, pistol-caliber lever-action rifles and either double-barrel or exposed-hammer pump shotguns.

There are three classes of firearms: Modern, which means a pistol having adjustable sights such as a Ruger Blackhawk or a Colt New Frontier; Traditional, which is either an original or a reproduction of a pistol with fixed sights such as a Colt Bisley or a Uberti reproduction of the Colt Single Action Army revolver; and Black Powder, which utilizes either a cap-and-ball revolver like a Colt 1860 Army revolver or a Traditional-class cartridge revolver using black powder for propellant. Black Powder class also requires that the shooter use black powder loads in the rifle and shotgun as well. The type of pistol and propellant determine the class in which you participate.

Lever-action rifles are represented by a wide variety ranging from original Winchester 1873 and 1892 models to current Marlin and Winchester carbines and the well-made Uberti copies of the original lever guns (which are increasingly becoming too valuable to shoot). The occasional Colt Lightning pump-action rifle can be seen, too.

For a shotgun, cowboy shooters are divided into two camps: double barrels or Winchester 97 pump shotguns. The pump gunners are only allowed to load two rounds at a time, to make both types of shotguns competitive, so the ability to reload quickly is more important than the type of gun. (As a **Wild Bunch** fan, I of course use a '97 Winchester.)

Most stages involve the use of two or more firearms in combination. The scenario presented at the beginning of this chapter is typical.

The shooter starts standing in a doorway, pistol in hand. (No quick-draw techniques are allowed.) At the timer's beep, the shooter raises his pistol and fires one shot at each of five metal plates, holsters his gun and moves to the prop horse, removes a shotgun from a scabbard, loads it, and fires at two knockdown targets, reloads, and shoots at two more. Shooting scenarios are designed either to be a representation of a historical event, or may be drawn from a western movie. The main purpose is to have fun shooting. Targets tend to be big and close. Adrenaline adds a significant level of difficulty without having to resort to tricky course design.

Dress is an important part of Cowboy Action Shooting, as competitors MUST dress in vintage costumes. No tennis shoes, baseball caps or running suits are allowed. Jeans, boots and a cowboy hat are the minimum, and most shooters go to great lengths to acquire an authentic look. Costume contests, for daily shooting wear and for a formal event, are just as much a part of Cowboy Action Shooting as the shooting. This is tied in with the requirement that every shooter MUST have an "alias." Some shooters choose a historic alias, such as "Billy Dixon" or "William Frank 'Doc' Carver." Others are right out of a B-movie western, like "Tex" or "Justin Case." Some aliases are regional in nature, like the "Durango Kid" or my own alias, "Mogollon Munk."

As noted above, the primary purpose of Cowboy Action Shooting is to have fun. The opportunity to dress up in western clothes and shoot old guns in frontier scenarios is what attracts so many people to the sport. Winning is secondary to participation. In fact, at all major cowboy matches, the great bulk of prizes awarded are not based on skill but random chance. A beginning shooter at End of Trail has as much chance of winning a Colt Custom Shop Single Action Army as does the class winner. Cowboy shooters do not want to go the way of IPSC and become sponsor/major-cash-prize oriented. This emphasis on participation as opposed to winning allows shooters of all skill levels to feel comfortable competing in Cowboy Action Shooting. Currently, about 20 percent of all cowboy shooters are either female or juniors, and these numbers increase every year. Some matches encourage family participation by having male-female or parent-child team stages, and all matches have classes for women, junior and senior shooters.

The hurly-burly of the typical cowboy shooting event, in this case, Winter Range – the National Championship of Cowboy Action Shooting.

If you take life so seriously that you're afraid to look a little silly, if a child no longer lives inside you, then Cowboy Action Shooting might not be your game.

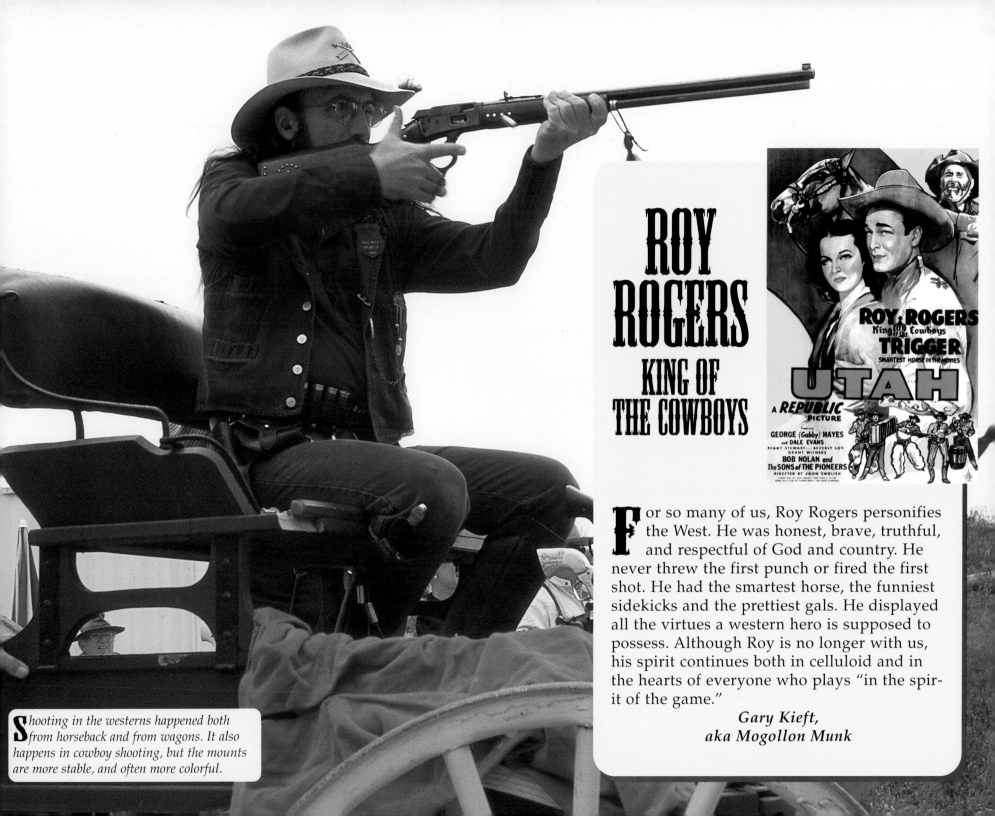

ROY ROGERS
KING OF THE COWBOYS

ROY ROGERS
King of the Cowboys
TRIGGER
SMARTEST HORSE IN THE MOVIES

UTAH

A **REPUBLIC** PICTURE

GEORGE (Gabby) HAYES and DALE EVANS
PEGGY STEWART · BEVERLY LOY
GRANT WITHERS
BOB NOLAN and
The SONS of THE PIONEERS
DIRECTED BY JOHN ENGLISH

For so many of us, Roy Rogers personifies the West. He was honest, brave, truthful, and respectful of God and country. He never threw the first punch or fired the first shot. He had the smartest horse, the funniest sidekicks and the prettiest gals. He displayed all the virtues a western hero is supposed to possess. Although Roy is no longer with us, his spirit continues both in celluloid and in the hearts of everyone who plays "in the spirit of the game."

*Gary Kieft,
aka Mogollon Munk*

Shooting in the westerns happened both from horseback and from wagons. It also happens in cowboy shooting, but the mounts are more stable, and often more colorful.

"It ain't like it used to be...
but it'll do."

CHAPTER ONE

"ONCE UPON A TIME IN THE WEST..."

Cowboy Action Shooting continues to grow by leaps and bounds. There are now clubs in all 50 states. Along with the rapid growth of the sport, participants are becoming more historically oriented. As a result, the "Hollywood Cowboy" look is being replaced by a more authentic portrayal of our western heritage.

Overall, Cowboy Action Shooting is evolving into a sport with more emphasis on participation, traditional firearms, traditional shooting technique and authentically styled leather and clothing predominating the ranges.

Back in 1979, a few IPSC shooters were sitting around the clubhouse after a match, talking about guns. The conversation got around to the classic western movie, *The Wild Bunch*, and the guns used in it. The various shooters present reflected on the single-action revolvers that were gathering dust in the rear of everyone's safes. It was decided to stage an action match in the flavor of the *Wild Bunch* movie, using those single-action pistols, lever-action rifles and old shotguns.

After a couple of false starts, the first cowboy action match was held in December 1979. About 25 shooters attended and everyone enjoyed the casual atmosphere. It was decided to have a similar match about every three months thereafter. These cowboy action matches were becoming so popular that three of the principals – Gordon Davis, Bill Hahn and Harper Creigh – actively pursued a two-day event.

In April 1982, the first two-day cowboy action match was held. This was the genesis of End of Trail, which attracted about 75 participants; the next year, about 125.

Based on this level of interest, End of Trail was incorporated into a non-profit corporation. By 1988, interest in Cowboy Action Shooting had grown, and the sport was starting to spread to other areas. Thus, a need to establish guidelines to ensure continuity of the sport became apparent.

An organization was developed to promote the interest in and growth of Cowboy Action Shooting – SASS, the Single Action Shooting Society. The first SASS member was signed up in February, 1989; none other than Harper Creigh, now alias Judge Roy Bean. SASS drew up a set of guidelines for new clubs to use, and ran End of Trail.

Over the years, SASS has grown from a loose group of cowboy shooters to become the parent organization with over 20,000 individual members. Cowboy shooting clubs, following SASS guidelines, have been started in all 50 states and in five foreign countries.

For the first few years, End of Trail was an unclassified match. Adjustable-sighted Rugers won the match the first two years, then a fixed-sight Colt won the third year. After this, "The Wild Bunch" decided some degree of classification would be beneficial. The first classes established for Cowboy Action Shooting were Traditional, Modern, and Woman's classes.

In 1987, Black Powder class was added, requiring competitors to use percussion revolvers and black powder propellant in their rifle and shotgun ammunition. Eventually, this class evolved into Black Powder Cartridge class, using

traditional pistols in lieu of percussion guns. In 1994, Winter Range reintroduced percussion pistols into the main stages with the "Frontiersman" class. SASS gave conditional approval to this class in 1994 and 1995, and restored it to class status in 1996.

The Senior class was introduced in 1987. Since then it has steadily grown, so in 1995 SASS raised the qualifying age to age 65, to reduce the administrative load. In 1988, a Junior class was authorized. By 1994, Junior was subdivided into Young Adult (17-20 years) and Junior (12-16 years). By 1994, growth in Women's class forced a split into two categories, Women's Traditional and Women's Modern classes.

The Duelist class, introduced at the 1993 Winter Range and formally adopted by SASS in April 1993, allowed the shooter to adopt the traditional one-handed pistol shooting stance without being handicapped. Duelist has rapidly grown into one of the more popular classes.

SASS saw the creation of another major Cowboy Action Shooting Event in 1992, not to rival End of Trail, but to compliment it. Winter Range was founded by Jim (William Bruce) Rodgers, Steve (W. F. "Doc" Carver) Chapman, Gary (Mogollon Munk) Kieft, Bob (Buckshot Robert) Rainwater and a few other hearty souls, who wanted to see a major match that offered more shooting and was more shooter-oriented than End of Trail. They formed the Arizona Territorial Company of Rough Riders in the fall of 1991 to orchestrate just such a match.

The first Winter Range was held at Ben Avery Shooting Range outside of Phoenix, Arizona, in

Participation at SASS events has increased dramatically since its first match held in December of 1979 with 25 shooters.

Vaquero to lawman, schoolmarm to saloon girl, many participants like to adopt a persona, complete with a history, accouterments and costuming. You can keep it as simple or make it as elaborate as you wish.

February 1992. There were 165 participants who attended that inaugural match, which also introduced the Plainsman event and the Mounted Shooting event (as an exhibition). In 1993, Winter Range introduced the Duelist Class as a main event category and Mounted Shooting became an exciting new side event. A special team event commemorating famous cinematic shootouts was added in 1994, commencing with the final scene from the movie *The Wild Bunch*, including a 1917 Browning water-cooled machine gun supplied by Dillon Precision Products. The 1995 team event honored the movie *Tombstone*, as many Cowboy Action Shooters were extras in the film.

Winter Range continues to offer more shooting opportunity. In 1995, the Frontiersman percussion revolver class was reintroduced, and appears to be headed for a revival with renewed support from match directors, the shooting industry and the competitors.

Cowboy Action Shooting continues to grow. Five years ago there were only four or five regional events and one world-class event; now, participants can attend the National Championship at Winter Range, the World Championship at End of Trail and several dozen smaller major matches in the United States, Canada, Europe, and Australia.

With the evolution of the sport came the first classes for Traditional, Modern, Seniors, and Women. Pictured above is John Hansbury, 92 years young, AKA "Cactus Jack."

Mounted shooting began as an exhibition to entertain competitors while scores were being tabulated. Increased interest in mounted shooting led to the creation of the Cowboy Mounted Shooting Association (CMSA).

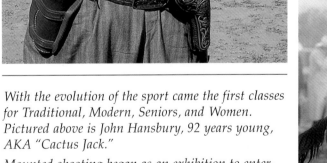

The ruling maxim for the cowboy shooter is that it's not how good you shoot, it's how good you look when you shoot!

CHAPTER TWO
GETTIN' SASSY

SASS, the Single Action Shooting Society, was formed in August of 1987 from the success of the End of Trail Cowboy Action Shooting Event. End of Trail heralded the rapid growth of Cowboy Action Shooting, and it was recognized that a national sanctioning body was needed to provide a standardized set of guidelines. The rules for End of Trail were adopted and assembled into a handbook for shooters. Next, it would be necessary to establish for individuals and clubs to join the governing body as members, and establish a registry for the shooting aliases of the individual members and of clubs complying with SASS guidelines. Finally, a newspaper for members was needed to provide a schedule of events, results of matches, relay rule revisions, plus provide a forum for articles and editorials of interest to the membership.

SASS signed up its first member, Harper Creigh, in February 1989. By the end of 1999, membership is expected to exceed 30,000. Clubs following SASS guidelines exist in all 50 states and in five countries.

The whole concept of Cowboy Action Shooting as a competitive sport is to have FUN! Stage and event winners are recognized with trophies and awards, but any/all prizes are given away by random lottery to all participants. Thus, any competitor can win a firearm, gunsmith action job, or whatever other prizes have been arranged for by the match directors or donated by sponsors.

"The spirit of the game" is the phrase that best describes competition in Cowboy Action Shooting. Everyone is encouraged to participate, but also to participate in such a manner as to try to do your best, without trying to outsmart or evade the meaning or intent of a course. If a stage requires you to pour a shot of "whisky" into a shot glass and yell "I'm your daisy" before firing a shot, then that's what you do. Shooters are encouraged to shoot the stage in the spirit in which it was designed. If someone seeking a competitive edge were to not pour the ersatz whisky and bellow the appropriate phase, he would be heavily penalized.

(Not to mention being socially ostracized with a dull ostracizer!)

The concept of "the spirit of the game" continues into firearms modifications, scoring and just being a cowboy shooter in general. If you can't participate without bending the rules to extract additional advantage, then you won't be invited back. We're all here to shoot and have fun. Winning is secondary to participation.

SASS recognizes the people who by their level of commitment personify "The spirit of the game" with a variety of awards. "Regulators" are those individuals who undertake the hands-on work of SASS, building props, registering shooters, repairing and building targets, and the like. Regulators are recognized with distinctive badges, which are awarded once a year at End Of Trail. For those who truly distinguish themselves as advocates of Cowboy Action Shooting, SASS has additional awards. The Spirit Award is a limited edition R. C. Merrill bronze for individuals who exemplify the spirit of the game. So far, only nine Spirit Awards have been issued.

For the rare individual who, in spite of many obstacles, perseveres on behalf of Cowboy Action Shooting, SASS has the "True Grit" Award. This award recognizes those who overcome personal injury, hardship and pain to contribute to Cowboy Action Shooting. As of 1995, the True Grit Award has only been issued twice. The Top Hand Award is issued annually to the person who has not only promoted the sport of Cowboy Action Shooting, but has had a major impact in the development of the sport. "Top Hand" was the highest accolade a cowboy could earn in the days of the Old West. Today, this award recognizes this same quality of talent, devotion and commitment to Cowboy Action Shooting.

Finally, SASS remembers its fellow shooters called to the last roundup. "God's Posse," a bronze memorial, is SASS's way of honoring and remembering its members who have passed away.

Cowboy Action Shooting is a very social event, with a close feeling of camaraderie. Most major events offer activities involving participants and their families beyond the shooting. Since dress is considered nearly as important as shooting, costume contests are another competitive outlet in Cowboy Action Shooting. Costume competition is divided into two major categories; working costume, which is based on a shooter's attire during the actual shooting, and formal costume, which is usually held after hours in conjunction with other evening festivities.

Formal costume is divided into men's, women's and junior classes, which are further subdivided into several different categories. At

Costuming can be a major component of cowboy action shooting, but it isn't necessary to spend big bucks on it unless you want to. Jeans, a long sleeve shirt, a hat and a pair of boots are all you need.

some events, the formal costume competition has evolved into a character portrayal, allowing the participant to display a persona as well as apparel. Costume competition has become pretty fierce over time. Small details like types of stitching, dates of money in pockets, or construction materials can separate first place from the also-rans.

Other social aspects of Cowboy Action Shooting include cowboy poetry reading, Dutch oven or chili cooking, dancing, and just carousing with friends and family. For most participants, the social aspects and camaraderie are more important and more memorable than the shooting.

ALIAS

Another critical adjunct to Cowboy Action Shooting is the alias. Every cowboy shooter MUST have a shooting alias to compete under. All administrative work, awards and prizes are done using the alias, not a participant's actual name. This is done to enhance the western flavor of Cowboy Action Shooting, and to give participants a feeling of role playing during an event. SASS is the official repository of shooting aliases. When individuals become SASS members, they can register their aliases at that time.

Duplicate aliases are not allowed. Many potential aliases, especially historical or fictional characters, are already taken. However, both historical research and writers' imaginations will continue to provide alias material for a long time to come. Many participants opt for humorous or geographically relevant aliases. Puns in particular abound among shooters' aliases.

The spirit of the game is to have fun and to participate in such a manner as to do your best – winning is secondary to participation.

Listed is a smattering of randomly chosen Cowboy Shooting aliases from among those already registered with SASS (in random order): IONA GUN • TEX • JUDGE ROY BEAN • CHOCTAW • DURANGO KID • ISLAND GIRL • CLAUDIA FEATHER • THE MAJOR • ROWDY YATES • TUTLER • EL RUBIO • DAKOTA ROY • LITTLE BIT OF WYOMING • HONDO • BUTCH CHASTITY • C. S. FLY • DUST DEVIL • NAT LOVE • MIDWAY • RINGO • GATLIN' • CHATO • PAT GARRETT • DARN IT DARR • BUTCH CAVECHEE • SISTER SARA • JUSTIN CASE • CASSIE REDWINE • EL TEJANO • GILA SLIM • DESERT ROSE • RAMBLIN' ROSE • HIPSHOT

In addition to acting as an alias registry, SASS performs other valuable tasks that make membership worthwhile. SASS is the parent organization of Cowboy Action Shooting, providing guidelines for the sport and overseeing changes in these guidelines. The SASS publication, *The Cowboy Chronicle*, includes match results, information on upcoming events, and articles of a historical or competitive nature. SASS also provides assistance to help form new clubs, and assist approved clubs with advertising and prizes for their regional matches. It benefits both the individual shooter and the club to be associated with SASS. So if you aren't a member, JOIN! If you are a member, upgrade to life membership. SASS is the glue that holds Cowboy Action Shooting together. Without it, the sport probably wouldn't exist. So, you support SASS, and SASS will support you.

Right – Non-shooters are equally encouraged to dress in period costumes.

Facing page – Cowboy Action Shooting is suitable for the entire family, regardless of age or gender. This terrible trio spans three generations of the Furr family.

Formal costume is divided into men's, women's and junior classes, which are further subdivided into several different categories. At some events, the formal costume competition has evolved into a character portrayal, allowing the participant to display a persona as well as apparel. Costume competition has become pretty fierce over time. Small details like types of stitching, dates of money in pockets, or construction materials can separate first place from the also-rans.

24

REX BELL

MONOGRAM
PICTURES
presents

REX BELL
in "DIAMOND TRAIL"
with FRANCES RICH

Directed by HARRY FRASER
Produced by TREM CARR
Story by SHERMAN LOWE

University of Iowa football hero George Beldam appeared in his first film, "Girl-Shy Cowboy" in 1928. His last film appearance was in "Lone Star" in 1951, three years before he was elected lieutenant governor of Nevada. Rex appeared in 35 films during his career.

George Beldam, aka "Rex Bell"
October 16, 1903 – July 4, 1962

*M*ovement is often required during shooting stages – note that the handguns are holstered, the shotgun is open, pointed downrange, and no fingers are on the trigger. Safety first, last, and always.

Prairie Weet, looking like a cowgirl from the 101 Ranch, engages a couple of shotgun targets.

HERB JEFFRIES
THE BRONZE BUCKAROO

I discovered Herb Jeffries when I was a kid growing up in Baltimore. It was a revelation and an inspiration to discover that there was a black movie cowboy to be my hero. At the time, I never dared believe that someday I would meet Herb Jeffries, let alone become friends with him. Herb saw the lack of cowboy movies with all-black casts. So, he rounded up some modest backing and started making movies. His films used the same B-movie scripts of the time, but the entire cast was black. After making four westerns, Herb joined Duke Ellington's Band, which put a halt to black singing-cowboy films. Herb Jeffries, The Bronze Buckaroo, remains the only black singing-cowboy movie star. I am proud to call him my friend.

Madison Walker, aka Nat Love

These two beautifully attired ladies stop to converse while shopping on Sutlers Row, a group of retailers who offer everything from horse tack to fine garments.

CHAPTER THREE

SAFETY, COWBOY ETIQUETTE AND SHOOTING TECHNIQUE

As in every other shooting sport, most rules are drawn up to prevent death, dismemberment or grievous bodily harm from occurring to either participants or spectators. Additionally, Cowboy Action Shooting has some codes of conduct unique to this sport.

Most Cowboy Action Shooting events are held at what is called a "cold" range. This means that guns are unloaded and long gun actions are open whenever the shooter is not on the firing line. When shooting a stage, a five-second penalty will usually be incurred if the shooter sets down a long gun with the action closed. Also, when you finish shooting a stage, be sure to inspect both the chamber and the magazine to be sure a firearm is empty.

At one major match, I witnessed an instance where a round hung up on the follower of an 1873 rifle, unnoticed by both the shooter (in his first big match) and the experienced individual who was shepherding him through the stages. Back under the covered area of the range, the shooter closed the open action and squeezed the trigger to drop the hammer, preparing to case the firearm. Everyone was surprised when the gun discharged. Fortunately for all involved, the shooter was pointing the muzzle in a safe direction, and no one was hurt.

This brings us to the next aspect of shooter etiquette, which is muzzle awareness. On the line, most ranges use a 170-degree rule, meaning that if the muzzle of the firearm being held by the shooter is not pointed downrange, some sort of penalty will be incurred. This is one the most serious safety infractions, and the usual penalty is to be disqualified from that stage. Under some circumstances, this infraction may get a participant ejected from a match.

The only more serious safety infraction that can happen is an accidental discharge (AD). An AD is defined as any occurrence of a firearm discharging when not under control. At most matches, if an accidentally discharged bullet impacts downrange at a distance greater than five feet from the shooter, no penalty is incurred. If the point of impact is within five feet of the shooter, or impacts past the 150/170 degree plane, the shooter will at least be disqualified from that stage, and possibly ejected from the match.

Dropping a gun is a major *faux pas*. If this occurs, the competitor will not be allowed to recover the firearm. The timer operator or some other designated stage official will retrieve the firearm, clear it, and then, depending upon the circumstances, some sort of penalty will be assessed. Usually, accidental discharges and dropped firearms are the result of entry-level participants suffering from the competitive equivalent of "buck fever."

There are other serious breaches of cowboy etiquette that can incur the wrath of range officials. If a loaded round is dropped during a stage, do not pick it up. It is considered "dead," and a replacement live round must be loaded from the body of the shooter. An attempted retrieval during the stage could result in breaking the 150/170-degree muzzle rule.

Handling firearms behind the firing line is another example of socially unacceptable behav-

ior. If you want to examine someone's firearm, either do so at a designated safety area or back in the parking lot. No matter how safe you are, people don't take kindly to gun handling behind their back.

Consuming alcohol during range hours is strictly prohibited. Alcoholic beverages can and often do add to the post-shooting festivities, but only after everyone is finished shooting and all firearms are put away.

At most cowboy events, shooters proceed through the various stages in groups known as posses. Each posse is responsible for running itself through each stage. Someone must run the timer, count misses, record scores, pick up brass, and perform all of the other activities essential to getting through a stage. As a participant, it behooves you to learn how to do all of these various things, and to do your fair share of them. Don't abandon your posse at a stage just because you've shot it. Stick around and help process the other shooters through the stage. Run the timer. Record scores (only if you have neat handwriting!). The more people who help run a stage, the faster and smoother everything goes.

Mounted shooting requires its own set of safety quide-lines. See Chapter Eleven for more information.

TIDBITS OF TECHNIQUE AND OTHER COWBOY TRIVIA

You can derive almost as much benefit from dry firing as from live practice. At home, you can practice gun handling, reloading, reholstering and drawing a second gun from its holster. Make up some dummy rounds using the same components as your live ammo, and then be sure to render them easily identifiable. Drill a couple of holes through each case, or dip them in dychem (repeating as it wears off), or use nickeled cases. Then try reloading in different ways, and see which style is fastest for you. Let's face it, the large, close targets used for cowboy shooting don't necessitate a great quantity of paper-punch-

John Shaw ("Idaho John"), a highly analytical competitor, demonstrates his 1.5-second transition from first pistol to second. The trick is to reholster the crossdraw revolver while simultaneously drawing the second gun from the strong side holster – the very definition of economy of movement.

ing. However, you can really polish up your gun handling with dry practice at home.

The new Ruger pistols, which have a two-screw lockwork and utilize transfer bar technology, do not have a half-cock notch in the hammer. Opening the loading gate disengages the cylinder locking bolt, allowing the cylinder to rotate for loading and unloading. On the Colts, you must retract the hammer to the half cock notch in order to unlock the cylinder for loading and unloading.

An idiosyncrasy with Rugers is that if you rotate the cylinder until you hear the hand click on the ratchet, the chamber is advanced too far to eject the fired case. You then have to cycle the cylinder completely around again to get to the fired case. If you let go of the hammer while cocking, the cylinder will advance one chamber. Again, you will have to cycle the cylinder past the other five chambers to reach the live round you skipped. Colt revolvers, on the other hand, line up the chamber with the loading port when the hand clicks on the cylinder ratchet. However,

letting the hammer slip on a loaded Colt will still advance the cylinder by one chamber, forcing you to race around to get back to the loaded chamber. Very embarrassing.

One other useful tidbit of information, especially for shooters unfamiliar with the single-action revolver, is to cock the hammer of the gun with the weak hand. It is much faster and much safer than cocking the gun with the strong hand, as the shooter has better control over the gun.

The Henry rifle has a couple of peculiarities of which shooters should be aware. The cartridge follower protrudes from the bottom of the magazine tube. If you grasp the rifle in a normal manner, the follower will stop when it hits your hand; when this happens, there is no pressure on the cartridges to feed them into the lifter. The result is a lot of energy expended without anything going "bang." Be sure to "pinch" the magazine, creating a tunnel for the follower to slip through. Additionally, DO NOT let the follower slam down on a loaded magazine. I have witnessed one blown Henry rifle when the shooter accidentally let the follower slam down on top of cartridges. Not much fun.

Another potential problem that can be encountered with the toggle-action rifles is one of mixing calibers. If you are shooting pistols in .45 Colt, and a rifle in .44-40, be sure not to inadvertently load any .45s in the magazine. If this happens, then the firearm will jam, as the taper in the cartridge lifter will not allow the cartridge to be removed from the gun. The only way to clear the firearm is to remove the sideplate and then remove the rounds from the magazine. This same type of problem can also occur with .44-40 ammunition in a 1873 Winchester chambered for .38-40.

Newer 1894 Marlins and 1894 Winchester Carbines suffer from a liability-lawyer-designed hammer block safety. Many, many times I have watched shooters pick up a rifle, go through all the proper motions, and not fire a single round. Somehow, during the staging of the gun, the safety got bumped on. Additionally, some models of Marlin lever actions have a folding rear sight. Sometimes, if a rifle is pre-staged in a scabbard, this style of sight can get folded down, presenting an inferior sight picture when shooting.

Stages requiring a rifle reload are uncommon, but expect to encounter one or two at any major match. For this limited use, most cowboy shooters rely on a vest pocket for reloads. The problem with bandoliers is that as you use up ammunition, they have a tendency to try to shift position around you. A web cartridge belt is the best way to carry extra rifle rounds, as it posi-

Above – Costume and equipment are critical. However, it is important to keep in mind the physical activities involved in Cowboy Action Shooting and to avoid encumbering oneself with accessories or props.

Left – Old West cowboys ran the risk of mixing .45 pistol cartridges with .44-40 rifles, as evident in this view of an Uberti Winchester 73 with both types of ammunition.

Facing Page – Cowboy Action Shooting doesn't stop because of rain. Have a slicker or an Australian drover's coat handy.

Cowboy Mounted Shooting requires equal parts horsemanship and gun handling ability. It's about as close to the silver-screen western as you can get.

tions the ammunition higher on the body so they are about the same level as the dismounted rifle, for quicker reloading.

One possible speed advantage to the exposed-hammer double-barrel shotgun is that the gun opens faster since you are not cocking the hammers mechanically during the opening process.

Most Cowboy Action Shooters use either a belt slide shotshell holder or a web waist belt to carry shotshells. The belt slide is the more convenient method, but the web belt, if worn above the pistol belt, is faster. This is because it holds the ammunition at about the same height as the receiver of a dismounted shotgun. The shells are closer to the breech of the gun and require less hand movement for a reload.

Guncarts can be basic and functional or elaborate and decorative. They come in all shapes and sizes and some come in the form of organic guncarts like Becky the burro, SASS member #1000.

One helpful fashion hint; do not wear a pocket watch while shooting. If you ever have to bend over during a stage, the chain may wrap itself around the hammer spur on your pistol, causing endless embarrassment. Historically, it did cause one Jim Courtright to pull up short in a shoot-out in Fort Worth, once upon time, where it caused him to settle for second place.

Also, don't burden yourself with superfluous equipment and accessories during a stage. The (infamous) pocket watch, bowie knife, derringer, etc., all add to costuming, but just provide more to drop or get in the way while shooting a stage. Remove them when preparing for a stage, and then afterwards restore your costuming.

GUNCARTS

When attending a major match, most participants rely on some sort of guncart to convey their firearms, ammunition, and other accouterments. These typically resemble what one would imag-

ine a 19th century golf cart would be like. Most guncarts are homemade, using lawn mower wheels and wooden construction. Some local artisans produce guncarts for sale at cowboy matches, and some shooters utilize a child's wooden wagon to haul their equipment around. Guncarts are assuming the status of art objects; some major matches give awards recognizing guncart design and uniqueness. One shooter, Logan by alias, has a burro named "Becky" perform as his organic guncart. SASS recently recognized her unique qualities when Judge Roy Bean bestowed membership #1000 on Becky.

A few small creature comforts can make participation in a cowboy match a much more enjoy-able experience. A chair or folding stool to sit on when between stages will be welcome by the end of the day. Cowboy matches always occur when it is either hot and dry or cold and rainy. There is no in between. Either way, an umbrella is a nice option to have for climate control. In the same regard, a jug of water will cut the trail dust in either hot or cold weather. Sun screen is a must in the summer, and bug repellent could be useful in some locales.

Cowboy Action Shooting doesn't stop because of rain. Have a slicker or an Australian drover's coat handy, and a large garbage bag to protect your gear. Gunsocks, such as sold by Dillon Precision, are very useful for keeping dust out of firearms actions when in your guncart. Other handy items to include in a guncart would be a screwdriver, gun oil, a wiping rag, a cleaning rod and bag for fired brass. Finally, some sort of shooting bag is very helpful to store your gear in. For an authentic look, a drywall hanger's bag offers a leather bottom, canvas sides, and is affordable and easy to find.

Being familiar with whatever firearm you choose is critical to safety and handling techniques, especially on a crowded firing line.

Facing Page – Faster! Faster! China Camp and Columbus D. Shannon go man-to-man.

TIM McCOY

A veteran of 89 films, a TV series, and WWII, Tim McCoy also toured with the Ringling Brothers' circus and started his own Wild West show. His first film was "The Thundering Herd" in 1925 and archive footage of Tim as Colonel Tim McCoy last appeared in the TV mini series "Hollywood" in 1980.

Top speed thrills amid a hail of BULLETS!

Tim McCOY in SILENT MEN

with FLORENCE BRITTON
MATTHEW BETZ ... WHEELER OAKMAN
DIRECTED BY D. ROSS LEDERMAN

A COLUMBIA PICTURE

CHAPTER FOUR

A GUN OF THE HAND, OR... CLASS REVOLVES AROUND A PISTOL

There are two primary classes for Cowboy Action Shooting: "modern" and "traditional." All other classes are either subdivisions of Traditional Class or are gender/age specific, and free of firearm limitations. What differentiates these two classes is the type of sights on the handgun. A "modern" handgun has an adjustable rear sight, while a "traditional" sixgun has a fixed rear sight. The traditional class (or one of its subdivisions) is the most popular, while Modern Class is frequently an entry-level class. With most handgun targets only about seven to 15 yards away, adjustable sights are unnecessary.

Most people who enter Modern do so because they use their handguns for other types of shooting, or they prefer the squared shapes and precision of adjustable sights. Conversely, the traditional cowboy shooter is trying to recreate the feel of shooting with original equipment, with all of its limitations.

Three groups of handguns are used in Cowboy Action Shooting: Colt single-action revolvers (and copies), single-action Rugers, and the various uniquely designed original single-action revolvers and their copies.

Colts, their clones, and Rugers are available with either fixed or adjustable sights. The most noticeable difference between the Rugers and the Colt types is the size of the respective firearms, and the presence or absence of a half-cock notch. The Ruger is noticeably larger in both grip size and in the frame than the Colt-type. This also implies a greater weight for the Ruger. Additionally, the new Rugers, with a transfer bar safety mechanism, do not have a half-cock notch in the hammer. Opening the loading gate disengages the cylinder locking bolt, allowing the cylinder to rotate for loading and unloading. On the Colts, you must retract the hammer to the half-cock notch in order to unlock the cylinder for loading and unloading.

A distinguishing characteristic of the Rugers is that if you rotate the cylinder until you hear the hand click on the ratchet, then the chamber is advanced too far to eject the fired case. You then have to cycle the cylinder completely around again to get to the fired case. This also applies to shooting a Ruger pistol. If you let go of the hammer while cocking, the cylinder will advance one chamber. Again, you will have to cycle the cylinder around past the other five chambers to reach the live round you skipped past.

There is no question that Ruger is the more durable of the two designs. Many quick-draw artists used to modify Ruger Blackhawks to a Colt-style profile. This explains why Ruger's new fixed-sight Vaquero revolver is in such heavy demand. Introduced in 1993, the Vaquero has taken cowboy shooting by storm. In the first two years, over 75,000 Vaqueros were sold, made in both .45 Colt and .44-40. Recently .357 Magnum was added, along with a Bisley version.

However, the physical demands of Cowboy Action Shooting are not so rigorous as to preclude Colts. Colt-type handguns are more commonly used for several reasons. First, many people get into cowboy shooting out of an interest in the historical aspect of the sport. These people often choose Colts (or copies) due to their histori-

cal significance. Next, the Colt-style guns are lighter and a little quicker to handle. Finally, some people may already have an original rifle in an older caliber that they wish to match.

TO COLT, OR NOT TO COLT: IS THAT THE QUESTION?

Colts offer an investment value, whatever the generation, in addition to their shooting value. And, an original Colt won't lose value from shooting it, unless you blow it up! However, their initial cost is much greater than the clones. The clones feel the same, shoot the same, and in some instances, all of the parts will interchange with a Colt. Additionally, if you want a specific style of Colt, such as a black powder frame, or an artillery style, it is likely available in a clone. If you could find the style you wanted in an original Colt, and it was in shootable condition, it could easily cost several thousand dollars. For this much money you could purchase an entire clutch of clones. Additionally, some of the Colt clones are available in the older, traditional calibers such as .38-40 and .32-20 as well as the more common .357, .44-40 and .45 Colt.

Two manufacturers dominate the Colt clone market, A. Uberti and Armi San Marco (ASM), both of Italy. They are sold by various importers under several different names, including the EMF Hartford (ASM), Cimarron Model P (ASM), U.S. Patent Firearms (Uberti) and American Arms (Uberti). Although both manufacturers offer simi-

The revolver embodies the classic image of the gunfighter. The showdown on Main street between larger-than-life heroes and villains, though of course all SASS gunslingers are heroes!

Facing Page – Quick-draw is not Cowboy Action Shooting, although many of the top quick-draw artists are also very competitive cowboy action shooters. Here, gunsmiths Bob James and John Phillips demonstrate their speed out of the leather.

lar products, there are some fundamental differences between the two. Uberti utilizes investment castings for most of its components, and has a passive safety built into the hammer on its revolvers. Armi San Marco makes its handguns from forged steel stock, and machines them on modern CNC equipment. For a safety, ASM uses an overlong cylinder pin that can be pushed back through the frame to physically block the hammer. Generally, Armi San Marco parts will interchange with genuine Colt parts (with some amount of normal fitting), and in the hands of a good gunsmith will tune up just like a Colt.

At the 1998 End of Trail, Colt unveiled its newest offering for Cowboy Action shooters, the Colt Cowboy. Colt Single Action Army revolvers have long commanded a high price. Insiders told us one reason for this was a deliberate effort (influenced by product liability attorneys) to price the gun out of the "shooter" category and into a "collectors-only" market; and because the Model P does require a large amount of hand fitting.

With the obvious popularity of the various "Colt clones" and the Ruger Vaquero (and, more important, their price ranges), Colt felt the market was ready for a less-expensive "Colt" single-action revolver. Achieving this would require liability resistant lockwork and changes to the design that would minimize the need for hand fitting.

The Colt Cowboy does all of this. A transfer bar and a frame-mounted floating firing pin took care of the first requirement, and investment castings of chrome-moly steel took care of the second.

At this time, the Colt Cowboy is only offered in .45 Colt, 5-1/2-inch barrel length, with color-cased/blued finish. Wisely, Colt retained the traditional half-cock notch and hard rubber grips of the Model P.

The last class of handguns, the original non-Colts, is probably the most intriguing. This class includes such classics as the Smith & Wesson break tops; the Merwin & Hulbert, with its Chinese key-ring puzzle design; and the Remington 1875 and 1890 models, just to name a few. Generally, these guns are for the hard-core historical aficionado or the serious gun collector.

Recently, the Colt-clone manufacturers have been paying increased attention to this market. The Remington 1875 model has been available for some time, as has the 1890 Remington revolver. Navy Arms has re-introduced the Smith & Wesson Schofield revolver, having lengthened the frame and cylinder to allow chambering in .45 Colt and .44-40. This should make for lightning-fast reloads, as long as a rim doesn't slip under the extractor star. Uberti is manufacturing these for Navy Arms. Production is slow, and the price is not insubstantial, but the Navy Arms offering is beautifully crafted, with color-cased hammer, trigger, trigger guard, barrel catch assembly, and a nicely blued frame, cylinder and barrel assembly. The sights are copies of the minuscule originals.

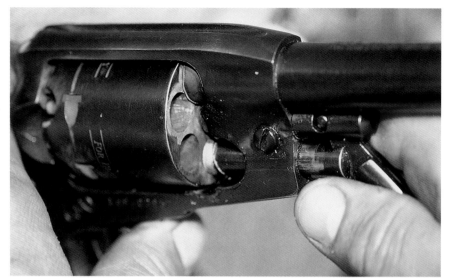

Two variations are offered, the 7-inch barrel cavalry model, with military markings, and the Wells Fargo model, equipped with a 5-inch barrel and Wells Fargo markings. A Cimarron Arms Schofield clone, courtesy of Armi San Marco, is also available in the same barrel lengths, and chambered for .45 Colt, and .45 Schofield. Keep in mind that all Armi San Marco firearms are manufactured of steel forgings and not investment castings.

BARRELS, THE LONG AND SHORT OF IT

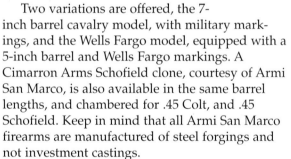

The length of barrel can have dramatic effects on the handling of a piece; it will effect the balance, the sight radius and the overall feel of a pistol. The good news is that as far as being competitive, none of this will have any real meaning, as the average pistol target is only seven to 15 yards distant. Most barrels will be in the traditional lengths of between 4-3/4 to 7-1/2-inches but can

The loading of a percussion revolver requires precision and patience. "A small ribbon of lead should be cut from the ball as it's seated. This press-fit is very important, as it seals off the powder behind the ball from the flash of an adjacent chamber going off. When a failure to seal the powder from an adjacent discharge occurs, it is called a "chain fire," which is spectacular to watch from a safe distance, but can be hard on the shooter."

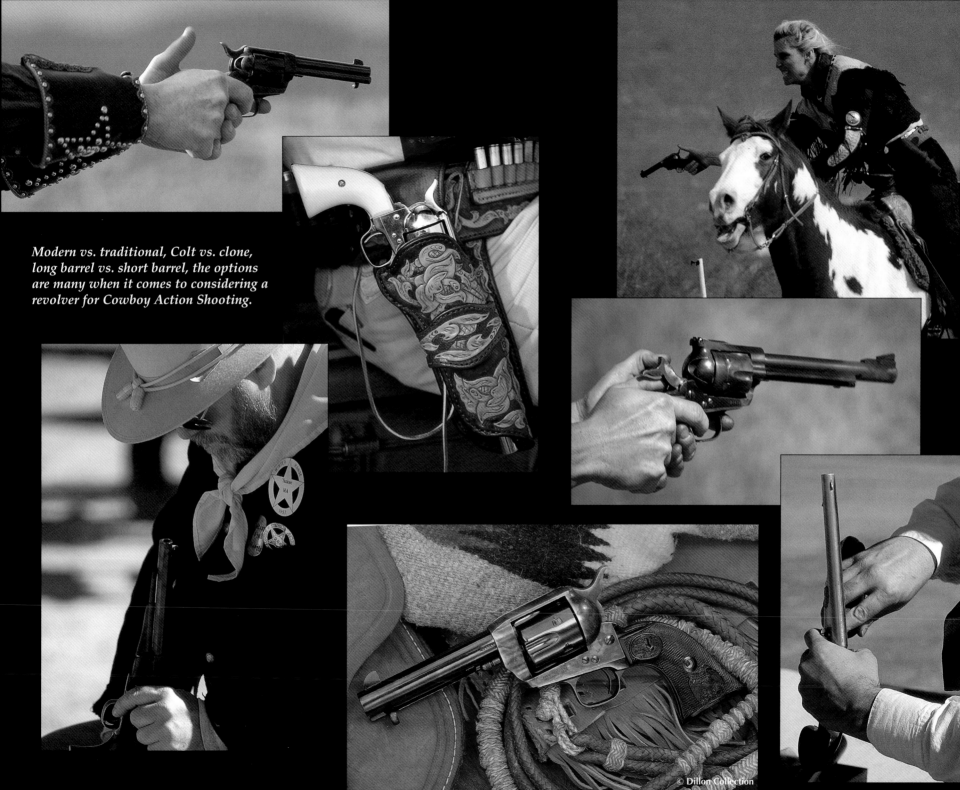

*Modern vs. traditional, Colt vs. clone,
long barrel vs. short barrel, the options
are many when it comes to considering a
revolver for Cowboy Action Shooting.*

© Dillon Collection

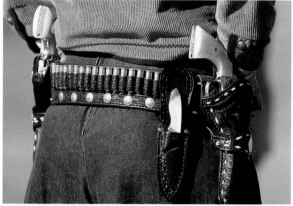

be anywhere from two- to 12-inches long. The longer barrel provides a greater sight radius, more weight out front to help curb recoil, and better balance. The drawbacks to longer barrels are that they are slower to draw and reholster, and for that time in between stages, they are heavier to cart about on your carcass. The shorter barrels can feel faster due to their lighter weight and reduced length, and are quicker to manipulate into and out of a holster. Besides, the shorter barrels better fit the mental image of the gunfighter. Get whatever length of barrel you like best; if it feels better or if it best suits the character or era you wish to portray.

One other useful tidbit of information, especially for shooters unfamiliar with the single-action revolver, is to cock the hammer of the gun with the weak hand. It is much faster and much safer, as the shooter has better control over the gun.

The choices are many when it comes to selecting a revolver. The same is true when it comes to how you choose to wear it.

Facing Page – Running Bare, a perennial top ladies' shooter, draws a bead on another iron plate.

CHAPTER FIVE

WINCHESTER '73 ... OR '92 ... OR '94 ... OR ?

The prospective competitor has lots of choices when considering which rifle to use for Cowboy Action Shooting. SASS rules require an exposed hammer, manually operated rifle chambered in at least .25 caliber, using a lead projectile at a maximum velocity of 1400 feet per second. With an exception to be addressed later, this means a lever-action rifle chambered in a pistol caliber.

IS YOUR RIFLE A CARBINE?

The first point to consider is barrel length. A carbine typically has a barrel length of 20 inches or less. A rifle will have a barrel of 24 inches or more, going out to 30 inches on some models. Shorter guns offer an advantage in ease of handling, such as maneuvering around stage props or extracting the gun from a scabbard. Plus, some people specifically wish to buy a carbine, either for aesthetic reasons, historical preference, or weight limitations.

The full-size rifles offer a longer sight radius and more forward weight for smoother movement when swinging the muzzle from target to

target. Also, for offhand shooting, the greater forward weight can be steadying. An 1873 rifle with a 24-inch barrel can weigh 8.25 pounds, and a Henry rifle can weigh 9.5 pounds. An 1892 Winchester carbine will weigh only 6.5 pounds.

Additionally, a rifle will hold more ammunition than a carbine. A 24-inch barreled rifle will typically hold 13 rounds in the magazine, while a 20-inch barreled carbine will hold only 10 rounds. The Winchester 94 Trapper only carries nine rounds in the magazine, equipped with its 16-inch barrel.

The best suggestion would be to spend some time handling various guns, and perhaps attend a match and try a few rounds through some. This will allow you to see what feels best to you.

TOGGLE VS. VERTICAL LOCKING BLOCK

As you handle different types of lever guns, you will notice that there are two predominant designs; the toggle action of the Henry, 1866 Winchester and the 1873 Winchester; and the

vertical locking block or blocks of the 1892 Winchester, the 1894 Winchester and the 1894 Marlin. Design-wise, there is no question, the vertical locking block designs are smoother and faster.

Most of the winning cowboy competitors use a lever gun of this design. The 1892 Winchester is now well represented in the firearms market. Via Navy Arms, Rossi offers rifles with half or full octagon barrels in addition to the line of round-barreled carbines. Armi San Marco of Italy offers an octagon barreled rifle through EMF in .357, .44/40, and .45 Colt. Even U.S. Repeating Arms offers an 1892 rifle, with a more subtle tang safety. The Rossi copies of the 1892 Winchester are somewhat rough to operate out of the box, but can be smoothed up easily, are quite accurate and are very affordable. 1995 saw the Rossi 1892 carbines offered in .45 Colt, and a return of .44-40. Finally, most shooters won't be able to tell any difference in the speed of operation among the different designs.

Toggle-action lever rifles are very popular

among cowboy shooters. The Henry, 1866 and 1873 Winchester designs represent the historical heyday of the lever gun. Shooters who wish to recreate a character from the era of 1860 to about 1890 will opt for one of these guns. Most of the toggle-action rifles in use are reproductions, because the originals have a collector value equal to if not greater than the cost of a reproduction. In addition, many originals are in less-than-pristine condition, having seen many years of hard use. And finally, the original Henry rifle and 1866 Winchesters were normally chambered for the .44

Henry Rimfire cartridge, a round which is no longer available.

Regardless of the name brand, all of the current Henry, 1866 and 1873 Winchester reproductions are made by A. Uberti of Italy. They are extremely well made, beautifully finished and very accurate. The only actual difference between them is the roll markings of the various importers.

There are a couple of peculiarities of the Henry Rifle to be aware of because the cartridge follower protrudes from the bottom of the maga-

zine. If you grasp the rifle in a normal manner, the follower will stop when it hits your hand; when this happens, nothing is putting any pressure on the cartridges to feed them into the lifter. The result is a lot of energy expended without anything going "bang." Be sure to "pinch" the magazine, creating a tunnel for the follower to

Arizona Billy Tilghman cycles his '73 Winchester as fast as he can. Just remember, it's hard to catch up to a miss.

The prospective shooter has lots of choices when considering which rifle to use for Cowboy Action Shooting. The best suggestion would be to spend some time handling various guns, and perhaps attend a match and try a few rounds through some rifles. This will allow you to see what feels best to you.

induce all sorts of stress in a shooting match, let alone an actual gunfight.

For this reason, one style of cartridge belt I strongly recommend against is the double-row belt, at least if putting different calibers of ammunition in each row. I know all about it. Gordon Davis sent me a beautiful latigo and web rig to try out, so I put .45 Colt in the bottom row, and .44/40 in the upper row. During a major match, a rifle reload was required while ensconced in a buckboard. So far I had shot the entire event clean. I polished off the first rick of rifle targets, then reached down *without looking* and proceeded to pluck ammo for the mandatory reload.

The Henry loaded up promptly, but after two more successful shots, the action wouldn't close, wouldn't eject, wouldn't do nothin.' So I set the rifle down, took the misses, and finished the rest of the stage. The stage over, I, my errant Henry rifle, and my Mini-Smith Screwdriver headed for the unloading area. You just would not believe how far you have to disassemble a Henry rifle just to get a .45 Colt cartridge out of the lifter. Tearing it apart on a hay bale during a thunderstorm was just icing on the cake. It was truly a chastening experience.

PITFALLS OF BUYING A "NEW" GUN

Problems exist with the majority of the current crop of Marlin and Winchester lever guns. Early Marlin rifles have "Micro Groove" rifling that is incompatible with all but the lightest of lead bullet loads. Micro Groove rifling consists of 12 shallow grooves that often fail to dig into a lead bullet enough to stabilize it. Exceptions to this were limited to the Marlin rifles chambered in .25-20, .32-20 and the Centennial Model Marlin in .44-40, all of which have conventional six-groove rifling. Cowboy shooters quickly picked the market clean of them. Recognizing this mar-

slip through. Additionally, DO NOT let the follower slam down on a loaded magazine. I have witnessed one blown Henry rifle when the shooter accidentally let the follower slam down on top of cartridges. Not much fun.

Another potential problem, actually more of an operator error, that can be encountered with the toggle action rifles is one of mixing calibers. If you are shooting pistols in .45 Colt, and a rifle in .44-40, be sure not to inadvertently load any .45 Colt in the magazine. If this happens, the firearm will jam, as the taper in the cartridge lifter will

Just as in revolvers, many rifle models have their own quirks in operation and staging procedures.

not allow the cartridge to be removed from the gun. The only way to clear the rifle is to remove the sideplate and then remove the rounds from the magazine. This same type of problem can also occur with .44-40 ammunition in a 1873 Winchester chambered for .38-40.

Historically, this problem occurred during a Texas Ranger battle with Indians in 1881. Ranger George Lloyd loaded a .45 Colt cartridge into his 1873 Winchester. Upon working the action, the oversize round jammed the gun. In the midst of the battle, George recognized the problem, took out his pocket knife, removed the sideplates, cleared the action of the offending cartridge, reassembled the firearm and resumed fighting. This type of "operator error" can

ket, in 1996 Marlin introduced the Model 1894 Cowboy, chambered for .45 Colt and equipped with a 24-inch octagon barrel with deep-cut rifling. This rifle was designed specifically for cowboy shooting.

The standard 1894 Marlin and the 1894 Winchester Trapper both suffer from an additional-liability-lawyer-designed hammer block safety. Many, many times at a match I have watched shooters pick up a rifle, go through all the proper

Above – Original rifles, in safe shooting condition, offer a decent investment value as well as being good shooters. Unless you blow up an original Colt Lightning (pictured), it probably won't decline in value.

motions, and not fire a single round. Somehow, during the staging of the gun, the safety got bumped on. Also, the 1894 Winchester Trappers I have seen frequently are cartridge-length sensitive. This is not unknown with the use of a short cartridge in a long action.

The new U.S. Repeating Arms version of the 1892 Winchester has a more aesthetically pleasing tang safety.

For a short period, Browning offered an 1892 carbine which is now highly sought after by cowboy action shooters. Like an original Winchester or Marlin, a limited-edition Browning also holds its value as an investment.

WHAT ABOUT AN ORIGINAL?

Original rifles, in safe shooting condition, offer a decent investment value as well as being good shooters. Unless you blow up an original Winchester or Marlin, it probably won't go down in value. The originals also offer a variety not found among current production rifles. A recent trend among competitors is to select an 1892 Winchester rifle chambered for .32-20 or .25-20. This firearm offers a long sight radius, steadying weight and non-existent recoil. However, no one currently offers the 1892 in a rifle smaller than .357 caliber.

Another unique original is the Colt Lightning, a slide-action, exposed-hammer rifle that is "lightning" fast. They are relatively fragile, but they are SASS-legal and they are different, which is of undefinable-but-definite value. Colt introduced the Lightning in 1884, after withdrawing their Burgess-designed lever-action rifle from the market due to pressure from Winchester (who threatened to introduce a competing line of handguns). Available in several frame sizes, the medium frame was the first size offered. It was chambered in .32-20, .38-40 and .44-40, and offered in both rifle (26-inch barrel, 15-round magazine capacity) and carbine (20-inch barrel, 12-round magazine capacity) variations.

Tang rear sights are allowed on rifles in all SASS shooting. For lever-action rifles, a few modern tang sights of indifferent quality were available, or else one could cruise the gun shows or the *Gun List* for a scarce original. Lyman has recently reintroduced its No. 2 Tang sight for Winchester and Marlin firearms. This should prove to be popular among cowboy shooters.

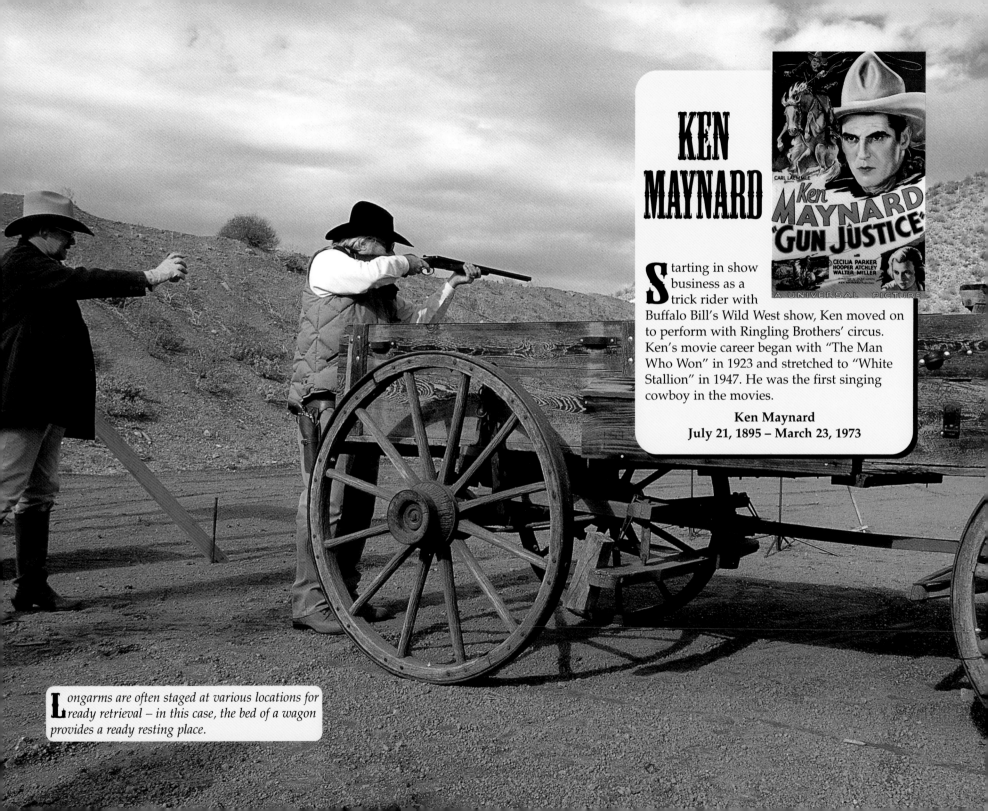

KEN MAYNARD

Starting in show business as a trick rider with Buffalo Bill's Wild West show, Ken moved on to perform with Ringling Brothers' circus. Ken's movie career began with "The Man Who Won" in 1923 and stretched to "White Stallion" in 1947. He was the first singing cowboy in the movies.

Ken Maynard
July 21, 1895 – March 23, 1973

Longarms are often staged at various locations for ready retrieval – in this case, the bed of a wagon provides a ready resting place.

BEN JOHNSON
THE GENUINE ARTICLE

Growing up in West Virginia, I of course watched the classic cowboy stars: Roy Rogers, Gene Autry and Hopalong Cassidy. But what really inspired me were cavalry movies in general and Ben Johnson in particular. I first journeyed to Montana when I was 19 years old to see the Custer battlefield and because of the cavalry movies. I returned to Montana, determined to get a job where I could ride a horse, after watching Ben Johnson ride in his western films. He rode like the true cowboy he was, and I was determined to do the same.

Mike Venturino, aka Iron Duke
Field Editor, Shooting Times Magazine

CHAPTER SIX
DRAWING A LONG, SMOOTH ONE

Choosing a shotgun for Cowboy Action Shooting can be no less confusing than selecting a rifle. There are three different types, two of which are only available on the used-gun market. The choices for a shotgun consist of a hammerless side-by-side, an exposed-hammer side-by-side, and an exposed-hammer pump gun. A few intrepid black powder shooters use the Winchester 1887 or 1901 lever-action shotguns, but these firearms are scarce, and are safe to use only with black powder loads.

HAMMERLESS DOUBLES

The hammerless side-by-side shotgun is the only SASS-legal shotgun for which current production is available. Shotgun targets are usually set quite close, typically 15 to 18 yards, so barrel length is not a major factor. However, you will occasionally find a flying clay pigeon or a team stage requiring shooting a log in two, which might favor a longer barrel with a bit of choke. Aesthetically, most shooters prefer a short-barreled shotgun; most factory sawed-off offerings

measure in the 20-inch range. It fits the image better, and that's just as important as targetability to most competitors.

The Brazilian IGA shotgun, currently imported by Stoeger, is readily available, of acceptable quality, and is very reasonably priced. Recently, an import from Baikal in Russia is turning up on the firing lines. Available in both 20- and 28-inch lengths, the Baikal doubles I have examined appeared to be sturdily built, with a utilitarian finish, and are competitively priced. Over the years, various companies have imported the Brno line of Czech side-by-side shotguns, which are of the highest quality.

EXPOSED-HAMMER DOUBLES

If your preference in smoothbores runs to the exposed-hammer double, or exposed hammer pump shotgun, you are forced into the used gun market. The Rossi Coach Gun, still available in Brazil, is no longer imported into the U.S., but is still the most readily available exposed-hammer double. At one time, they were relatively inexpensive, but demand by cowboy shooters has driven prices upward. Older shotguns are also available, but most of them have suffered from heavy use and marginal care. Be cautious. [*Editor's note: Having a side-by-side shotgun "double" on you is a sure way of getting a bloody nose, broken glasses and developing a world-class flinch. Buy a quality shotgun in good condition, please.*] One possible speed advantage to the exposed-hammer double is that the gun opens faster since you are not cocking the hammers mechanically during the opening process.

EXPOSED-HAMMER "PUMPS"

The same caveat about old hammer doubles also applies to the exposed-hammer pump shotguns. Represented by the 1897 Winchesters, and to a lesser extent by the Marlin exposed-hammer shotguns, pump shotguns offer a few perceived advantages over the doubles. SASS rules require shooters with pump shotguns to load only two into the magazine, with the chamber empty in the individual stages, but allow shooters to

stoke them fully during team events. Additionally, pump shotguns eject the fired round, whereas double-barrel shotguns are limited to having extractors, which partially pull the hull out of the chamber.

PICK WHAT YOU LIKE

No one type of shotgun is superior to another. End of Trail competition has had winners who used all three types. Find the shotgun you are most comfortable with. If it's a double, polish the chambers for easier extraction. For everything but log cutting, low-base dove and quail or target loads work fine for knocking down targets. For log cutting, and for some long distance team shoot targets, high-base #4 birdshot loads (the heaviest allowed under SASS rules) provide more punch.

"China Camp" (left) has the proper reloading technique down cold.

Facing page and inset – SASS rules require shooters with pump shotguns to start with two rounds in the magazine, chamber empty. Many shooters opt to restoke their 97s through the ejection port, as ably demonstrated by Claudia Feather, proprietress of Wild West Mercantile.

Choosing a shotgun for Cowboy Action Shooting can be no less confusing than selecting a rifle. There are three different types, one of which is only available on the used-gun market.

THE GOLDEN AGE OF TV WESTERNS

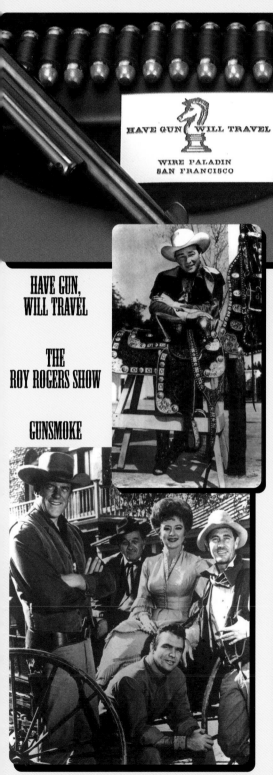

HAVE GUN, WILL TRAVEL

THE ROY ROGERS SHOW

GUNSMOKE

THE LONE RANGER

BONANZA

I was probably 12 or 13 before I realized that real cowboys wore black. Forget the conventional white-hatted good guy – the characters I most admired wore basic black.

It started with "Shane," the first movie I ever saw. To this day, Jack Palance's black-hatted malevolence still defines western wear for me.

In the '50s, the TV western became as popular as the big-screen epic. Here again, my youthful enthusiasm took impetus from Richard Boone's stylishly elegant Paladin character, who dressed in black from hat to boots.

Among the Cartwrights, my favorite on the Pondarosa was Adam, portrayed by Pernell Roberts. Always decked out in dark or black duds, he exuded cool competence in contrast to Hoss' down-home friendliness or Little Joe's easygoing popularity.

Now here it is, almost half a century later – Jack Palance won an Oscar for playing Curly, while The Duke and Richard Boone are long gone. But I still shoot in black hats to pay them homage.

Barrett Tillman,
aka Arizona Billy Tilghman

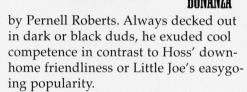

THE VIRGINIAN

THE CISCO KID

THE RIFLEMAN

CHAPTER SEVEN
BLACKSMITHING TO GUNSMITHING

In 1885, Bat Masterson penned an order to Colt ordering a .45 Single Action Army (SAA), requesting the factory to "make it easy on the trigger," along with a higher front sight, nickel plating and other embellishments. Today's Cowboy Action Shooters are no different. Some of the more popular modifications include reducing the trigger pull on all firearms, polishing the locking areas on rifles and shotguns for smoother, faster operation, and polishing the chambers on all firearms for faster extraction (especially on double-barrel shotguns and six-guns). But action work is not just to improve a gun's handling characteristics. Most action jobs will also increase the working life of a firearm. Problems like the barrel rubbing the cylinder face, soft indexing hands, and inadequate forcing-cone angle (which causes a revolver to spit lead) can be found in many new firearms, any one of which will accelerate wear. Another advantage to smoothing up an action is increased safety. For new shooters, especially women and juniors, the easier a firearm is to manipulate, the

less likely it will be mishandled, dropped or accidentally discharged.

LEE'S GUNSMITHING

This demand has led to the creation of a special class of "cowboy gunsmiths," who are familiar with the requirements of the sport. Lee's Gunsmithing is one of the best-known of these. Operating in Orange, California, Lee's is in the heart of Cowboy Action Shooting country. Performing tune-ups, repairs and action jobs on rifles, shotguns and pistols, Lee's Gunsmithing is always well represented in the winners circle. At the Master Gunfighter Shootout at the 1992 End of Trail, 16 of the 25 participants entrusted their guns to Lee's. Immediately after the event, Lee picked up four more of the participants. Lee's "Gunslinger" action job consists of the following: custom tuned springs, trigger job, timed and fitted hand, cylinder chambers chamfered and polished, hand-fitted and polished action, re-cut forcing cone, fit locking bolt, adjust loading gate and true up the barrel face. Lee's Gunsmithing

also does action jobs on percussion revolvers, lever-action rifles, double-barrel and 97 Winchester shotguns and derringers.

OGLESBY AND OGLESBY GUNMAKERS

Oglesby and Oglesby Gunmakers of Illinois is another shop that caters to all the arms work for cowboy shooters. Initially started as an IPSC-oriented shop, the proprietor, Bill Oglesby, has participated in Cowboy Action Shooting matches for several years, leading him to add cowboy gun work to his offerings. Oglesby and Oglesby also performs action work on rifles and shotguns.

BOB JAMES

Other cowboy gunsmiths choose to specialize in pistolsmithing. Arizonan Bob James has been tuning single-action Colts for more than 30 years. Bob made his name in Quick Draw competition, and entered Cowboy Action Shooting in its early years. Bob is a strong competitor in both sports and has the experience to tune guns

for either. Bob's work includes action jobs, changing calibers on Colt SAAs, adjusting barrels to alter the point of impact, and fitting exotic grips.

BOB MUNDEN

Bob Munden of Montana is one of the world's fastest quick-draw artists. He is listed in the Guinness Book of World Records, and puts on shooting exhibitions all over the country. He is also a consistently top competitor in the world of Cowboy Action Shooting. For years Bob has done his own action jobs, learning what stands up to the harsh demands of exhibition shooting. For the last several years he has performed action jobs and other gunwork for other shooters.

PEACEMAKER SPECIALISTS

Peacemaker Specialists was started by the long-time Colt authority John Kopec to offer parts and repair services for restoration of original Colt SAA revolvers. A few years ago, the California business was sold to Eddie Janis. Now, in addition to supplying parts and repairing original parts, Peacemaker Specialists also offers action jobs and trigger tune-ups for Cowboy Action Shooters.

ALPHA-TECH. COATINGS, INC.

Related to gunsmithing as far as firearm improvement is concerned is the application of rust-resistant and lubricative coatings. Teflon coating the internals of a firearm increases the

In 1885, Bat Masterson penned an order to Colt ordering a .45 Single Action Army (SAA), requesting the factory to "make it easy on the trigger," along with a higher front sight, nickel plating and other embellishments.

A good cowboy gunsmith can work miracles when it comes to smoothing up a lever-action rifle. But only you can make it hit the target.

working life of parts by providing greatly increased lubricity and a greater barrier to oxidation than bluing or nickel plating. Teflon coating the exterior of a firearm will provide a durable rust and heat resistant finish. The material being Teflon coated must be capable of being heated to at least 350 degrees, with 450 degrees being ideal.

Alpha-Tech. Coatings, Inc. is a firm familiar with applying Teflon coatings to firearms. They can apply Teflon coatings in almost any color, with matte black and matte silver being the most popular.

Above, right – A finely tuned Colt deserves handcrafted leather. Jack Stewart is one of the premier leathersmiths in the trade.

Left – It's not Brylcreem, but a little dab'll prevent a chainfire on your percussion revolver.

Facing Page – Custom long-range sights allow for best accuracy at maximum range.

CHAPTER EIGHT
FODDER FOR FIREARMS

The major dilemma a prospective cowboy shooter faces is what caliber or calibers to choose for rifle, pistol and shotgun. The attractive choice is to opt for a single caliber for both the rifle and the handgun. In theory, this allows the shooter to consolidate both rifle and handgun ammunition into one load, simplifying one's ammunition requirements. However, once most shooters gain some match experience, they start to tailor their loads for their specific requirements. Thus, even though a shooter may be using the same caliber, the net effect is to have two different calibers. The easiest way to get SASS-friendly ammunition is to make your own. About 80 percent of all cowboy shooters reload their own ammunition, as it is much less expensive than factory ammunition, and for some calibers, approved factory ammunition is just not available.

Don't let caliber availability limit your selection; get the firearms you are the most comfortable with, and then worry about the caliber. Many times the caliber selection among antique firearms will be very limited. With newer guns, caliber choice can be better, but local availability may still be restricted to a few choices. Imported firearms often must be ordered from various suppliers, who can usually get the firearm in whatever caliber is offered, provided you have sufficient patience.

MAIN-STAGE CARTRIDGES FOR RIFLES AND PISTOLS

.25-20 Winchester (.25 WCF)

Originally developed for the Model 1892 Winchester, the .25-20 cartridge was introduced in 1893. Based on the .32-20 case necked down to .257", the .25-20 is typically loaded with an 86-grain lead bullet. A flat trajectory and extremely low recoil are the hallmarks of this cartridge. This is the minimum rifle caliber allowable under SASS guidelines. Marlin has offered a short rifle chambered for .25-20, but it is handicapped with a half magazine.

Be aware that tolerance stacking may occur in the smaller calibers. A particular brand or lot of brass may not work in your particular firearm, due to neck or rim thickness. Test components in your gun before loading or purchasing any large quantities.

.32-20 Winchester (.32 WCF)

Introduced in 1882, the .32-20 cartridge was initially chambered in the 1873 Winchester rifle. Colt added this caliber to the SAA in 1884. The 1892 Winchester rifles in .32-20 have become very popular among Cowboy Action Shooters, who value the flat trajectory, low recoil and improved handling.

A caution with regard to the .32-20 is in order. A variety of bore diameters are out there, ranging from .311" to .316". For best accuracy you should measure the bore diameter, and use the appropriate size slug. 100- to 115-grain bullets are the most popular for .32-20. Recently, both Marlin and Browning have offered long guns chambered for this caliber. However, both manufacturers missed the market by offering guns equipped only with half magazines.

EMF offers its Hartford Model pistol in .32-20,

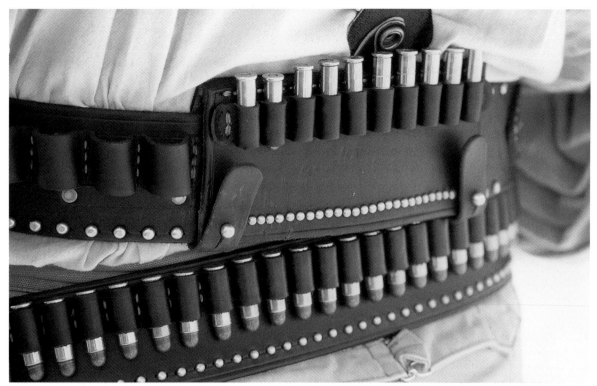

.38-40 Winchester (.38 WCF)

Winchester introduced this round in 1879 for its Model 1873 rifle. Colt added the caliber to its single-action pistols in 1884. There is very little practical difference between the .38-40 and the .44-40, mostly being the difference in bullet weights. The .38-40 typically uses a 180-grain bullet.

At this time, only original long guns are available in this caliber. None of the rifle manufacturers currently offer a rifle in .38-40. Among handguns, the EMF Hartford model is available in this chambering. A limited edition Ruger Blackhawk was offered with cylinders for both 10mm and .38-40 several years ago through Buckeye Sports.

Before reloading for any original .38-40 revolvers, be sure to measure both the bore diameter and the cylinder forcing cone dimensions. The First Generation Colts can have bores that vary from .400" to .408" diameter. Many of the earlier .38-40 revolvers shared barrels with the .41 Colt, which had a nominal bore diameter of .409". Failure to check this dimension can cause one to waste a lot of lead without producing any accuracy.

.44-40 Winchester (.44 WCF)

One of the oldest continually produced cartridges of all time, the .44-40 was introduced by Winchester in 1873 with their new steel-framed rifle, replacing the .44 Henry rimfire cartridge in the brass-framed 66 rifle. Colt adopted this round for the Single Action Army pistol in 1878, and eventually bestowed the moniker of "Frontier Six Shooter" on pistols chambered for this cartridge.

The .44-40 suffers from a problem of too many variations in dimensions, to a point where it's easier to treat it as two different cartridges: .44-40 for rifle and .44-40 for handgun.

In original long guns, most .44-40 bores run from .429" to .432". Current production rifles

and has problems keeping them in stock. Again, be aware that a particular brand or lot of brass may not work in your firearm, due to neck or rim thickness. Be sure to test components in your gun before loading or purchasing any large quantities.

.38 Special/.357 Magnum

The .38 Special/.357 Magnum caliber is probably the third most popular caliber among cowboy action shooters. Introduced by Smith & Wesson as a more powerful replacement for the .38 Long Colt cartridge, the .38 Special was officially chambered in Colt SAA pistols in 1930. The .357 Magnum cartridge was introduced by Smith & Wesson in 1935, and chambered by Colt in their SAA that same year. In pistols, the .38 Special is almost exclusively used, due to its low recoil and ease of obtaining components. Several different bullets are popular, with the 158-grain round nose, the 148-grain wadcutter and the 125-grain 9mm bullet sized to .357-.358" diameter being the favorites. For reloading during a stage, the 158 round nose and the 125 will reload faster, due to the convex nose shape. In rifles, most shooters use .357 brass in the lever actions, as few of those chambered in .357 will reliably feed .38 Specials. Most shooters use flat nose bullets like the 158-grain SWC or the 125-grain round nose flat tip bullet, to prevent a round going off in the magazine tube during recoil.

Many times the caliber selection among antique firearms will be very limited. With newer guns, caliber choice can be better, but local availability may still be restricted to a few options.

tend toward the .428-429" measurement. Just as important, the rifle chambers, on both original and current production guns, will accept loaded ammunition using either .428" or .429" bullets.

On original pistols, although the barrels may measure up to .432", the chambers will only accept ammunition loaded with a .425" bullet. Needless to say, this doesn't help accuracy. Most current factory .44-40 ammunition has .425-426" diameter bullets in order to ensure fitting in any chamber. Most currently produced .44-40 pistols have .427-.428" bores (although I have measured one Colt which had a .432" bore), and the chambers will accept ammunition loaded with a .428" bullet. The standard bullet weight for the .44-40 is 205-grains.

.44 Smith & Wesson Special

Introduced by Smith & Wesson in 1902 as an improvement over the .44 Russian cartridge, the .44 Special was first chambered in a Colt in 1913.

The late Elmer Keith did much to popularize this cartridge, after he discovered the hard way that the Colt SAA cylinders in .45 Colt were too thin to withstand his heavy loads using a 300-grain, .45-70 bullet. He then switched to the .44 Special cartridge, using his 240-grain Keith-style bullet and heavy loads of Hercules 2400 powder. The original factory round uses a 246-grain bullet, but most cowboy shooters either use a 240-grain bullet or the .429" diameter 205-grain bullet from the .44-40. Generally, the various rifles chambered for .44 Magnum will not reliably feed the shorter .44 Special cartridges, but it never hurts to try it for yourself.

Why is this cowboy smiling? Part of the reason would appear to be his collection of revolving pistols, bestudded holsters and rifle, and the ever-reliable Winchester 97 shotgun.

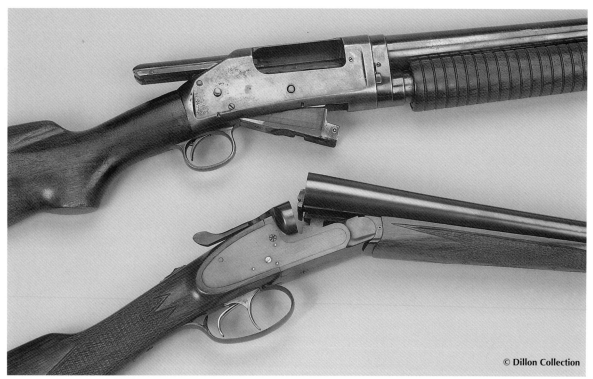

© Dillon Collection

.44 Magnum

Developed by Smith & Wesson in 1955, factory .44 Magnum ammunition is far too powerful for use in Cowboy Action Shooting. However, many shooters use reduced loads for use in their pistols or rifles for this sport.

A 240-grain bullet is the most popular for this caliber, but many reloaders use the .429" diameter 205-grain .44-40 bullet, because its lighter weight offers reduced recoil, and the traditional round nose flat point shape offers faster reloading while being safe for use in a tubular magazine.

The most common cowboy shotguns are the Winchester 97 pump (top) and various double-barrel coachguns (bottom).

.45 Colt (AKA .45 Long Colt)

Introduced in 1873 in the Colt Single Action Army revolver, the .45 Colt cartridge is another candidate for the oldest continually produced caliber in America. This is probably the most popular caliber for Cowboy Action Shooting.

The traditional bullet weight is 255-grains, but cowboy shooters are using anything from this weight down to the featherweight 155-grain bullets intended for compensated .45 ACP race guns.

This cartridge has a relatively small rim, which can cause extraction problems in rifles. This is the reason that no original lever actions were ever chambered in .45 Colt. Modern brass has a stronger head, and a shallow groove cut in the case head to give the effect of a wider extractor groove.

LONG-RANGE RIFLE SIDE MATCH CARTRIDGES

.30-30 Winchester (AKA .30 WCF)

Introduced in 1895 for the 1894 Winchester rifle, the .30-30 cartridge was the first American smallbore, smokeless, sporting cartridge. The initial load used a 160-grain jacketed bullet at a velocity of 1970 fps, but SASS rules require the use of lead bullets in long-range shooting events. Cast bullets in 150- to 170-grains are the most common, and the most accurate. The .30-30 is one of the most popular long-range repeating rifle cartridges, due as much to ready availability and lack of recoil as to its performance. Both new and used Marlin and Winchester lever actions are available, as well as the H&R Handi-Rifle for long-range single-shot class.

.30-40 Krag (AKA .30 Army)

The .30-40 Krag was the first smallbore, smokeless cartridge adopted by the United States Government. Introduced in 1892, this round was first chambered in a sporting arm by Winchester in 1893 for the High Wall rifle, and was more popular in the 1895 Winchester rifle. For long-range single-shot class, Shiloh Rifle Manufacturing Company offers their 1874 Sharps rifle in .30-40 chambering. In most .30-40 guns, a 200- to 220-grain lead bullet is necessary to obtain acceptable accuracy. The lighter bullets (150-175-grain) are not properly stabilized, and most old guns have long chamber throats meant for the longer projectiles.

.38-55 Winchester

Designed as a target round for the Ballard rifle, the .38-55 made its name first as a long-range single-shot target cartridge, then as a powerful hunting round in the big Marlin and Winchester lever actions. Factory loads used a (nominally) .375" diameter, 255-grain bullet at 1320 fps. Used firearms chambered for .38-55 are available in both single-shot and lever-action styles. However, be cautious as most of the older guns have bores of up to .382″ diameter, and most current cast bullets are only available in .375-.377″ diameter. Winchester made a few commemorative arms chambered for the .38-55 cartridge, and Shiloh Rifle Company offers their 1874 Model Sharps in this caliber. Browning has introduced its black powder silhouette rifle in the .38-55 cartridge, and Marlin is now offering a 336 lever-action rifle in this caliber. Some custom black powder silhouette rifles have been made in .38-55, usually with a barrel twist appropriate for the 300- to 350-grain lead bullets that are needed to put down a steel ram at 500 meters.

.45-70 Government (AKA .45-2-1/10″)

Tied with the .44-40 for the title of oldest continuously produced rifle cartridge, the .45-70 is still one of the most popular cartridges more than 120 years after its introduction in 1873. Developed for the Springfield trapdoor rifle, the .45-70 cartridge set the precedent for the popularity of all military rounds to come. By 1876, .45-70 was the most popular chambering in Sharps rifles, and was available in most other single-shot rifles of the era. The first lever-action available in .45-70 was the Whitney Model 1878 repeater, followed by the more popular 1881 Marlin rifle and the Winchester Model of 1886. The initial loading for the .45-70 used a .459″ diameter, 405-grain bullet propelled by 70 grains of black powder, producing a velocity of 1280 fps. In 1884, the bullet weight was increased to 500 grains after experience with the .45-80-500 cartridge in 1881. For Cowboy Action Shooting, most people use 300-

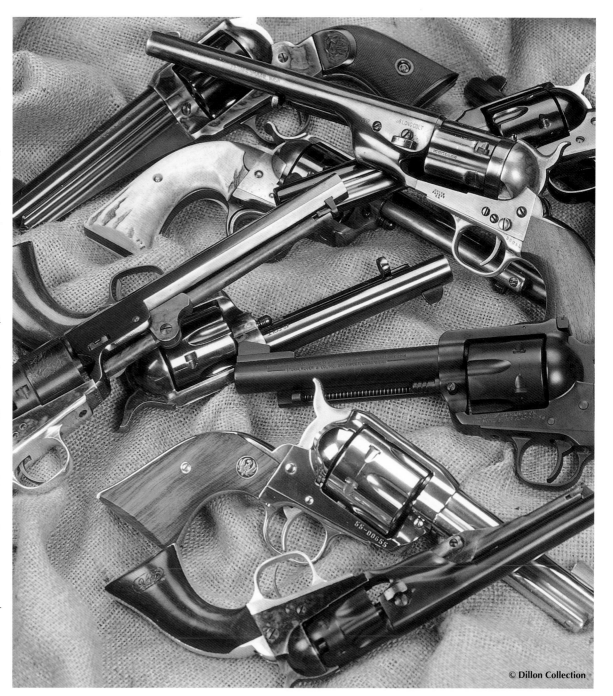

The variety of Cowboy Action Shooting revolvers is exceptional: cap and ball, original and replica cartridge guns, and modern single actions with adjustable sights.

© Dillon Collection

73

BILL PICKETT

Inventor of the rodeo sport of "bulldogging" (also known as steer wrestling), Bill Pickett was a rodeo cowboy whose career spanned more than 40 years. He was the first black cowboy ever inducted into the National Rodeo Cowboy Hall of Fame and the first black cowboy to appear in silent films.

Bill Pickett
December 5, 1870 – April 2, 1932

THE NORMAN FILM MFG. CO.
PRESENTS

BILL PICKETT
WORLD'S COLORED CHAMPION...
'THE BULL-DOGGER'
Featuring The Colored Hero of the Mexican Bull Ring
in Death Defying Feats of Courage and Skill.
THRILLS! LAUGHS TOO!
Produced by NORMAN FILM MFG. CO.
JACKSONVILLE, FLA.

grain lead bullets in lever actions, and 405-grain lead bullets in single shots. For knocking down silhouette rams at 500 meters, 500-grain bullets are needed, but most cowboy shooting is done at closer ranges using non-falling targets.

SHOTGUN LOADS AND SPECIFICATIONS

SASS requirements for shotguns specify a minimum of 20 gauge and a maximum of 10 gauge. Number 4 bird shot is the largest size allowed, and no magnum loads are permitted. For any shotgun shooting in a main stage, light target or dove and quail loads are quite sufficient for the reactive (knock-down) targets used. Occasionally, a thrown clay pigeon will appear in a stage, and the smaller (7-1/2, 8 or 9) shot sizes perform better. For team events, targets will sometimes require a heavier load. Some team events include cutting a log in two with shotgun fire, or knocking down bowling pins out to 25 or 35 yards. For this, high base (not magnum!) No. 4 or No. 6 shot works best.

Shot shells with impact-extruded hulls, such as the Winchester AA and other brands of target loads, typically pattern more uniformly, and extract MUCH easier from chambers than do the inexpensive game loads, which use a corrugated-tube hull. Also, the impact-extruded hulls reload easier and are more durable.

RELOADING FOR COWBOY COMPETITION

As in any shooting sport, most participants desire to perform to the best of their ability. In Cowboy Action Shooting, the equipment is fairly equal, so the most effective way to improve

Right – Bounty Hunter proceeds to convert perfectly good ammunition into dirty, empty hulls.

Facing Page – Though long out of production, the Model 1897 Winchester shotgun is a popular choice for cowboy action shooting.

one's performance is to practice. Factory ammunition is too expensive for most people to practice with and, in most calibers, is not suitable for cowboy shooting. A single-stage reloader requires an exorbitant amount of time to produce enough ammunition for a local monthly match, let alone having any ammo left over for practice. This is why about 95 percent of the cowboy shooters who reload use Dillon progressive reloaders. Dillon equipment requires less handling of the individual components, produces a loaded round with each stroke of the handle, and allows you to tailor your ammunition for your specific shooting requirements.

Before jumping into the reloading process, some preparation is necessary. Brass must be cleaned and inspected, and an appropriate bullet and powder must be selected. There are several reasons to clean your brass. First and foremost, this removes all grit and chunks that might scratch the cases, dies and the chamber of your firearms. Next, when brass is clean it is easy to inspect for damage or defects. Also, clean brass is easier to reload because there is less friction. And finally, clean brass looks pretty. For cleaning brass, a vibratory case cleaner is the most efficient method. You remove the lid, dump in dirty brass, re-attach the lid, hit the on switch and walk away. Come back in 1-1/2 to two hours, and it's done. The Dillon Case/Media Separator sorts the clean brass out of the media with a few cranks of the handle, and the brass is then ready for inspection.

All brass, even new factory brass, should be visually inspected prior to reloading. Flaws to look for in new brass include: missing flash holes, oversized primer pockets, case rims that are too thick and incorrect calibers mixed into a batch of brass. When inspecting used brass, problems and defects to look for include: crushed case mouths, cracks in case necks, debris (rocks or

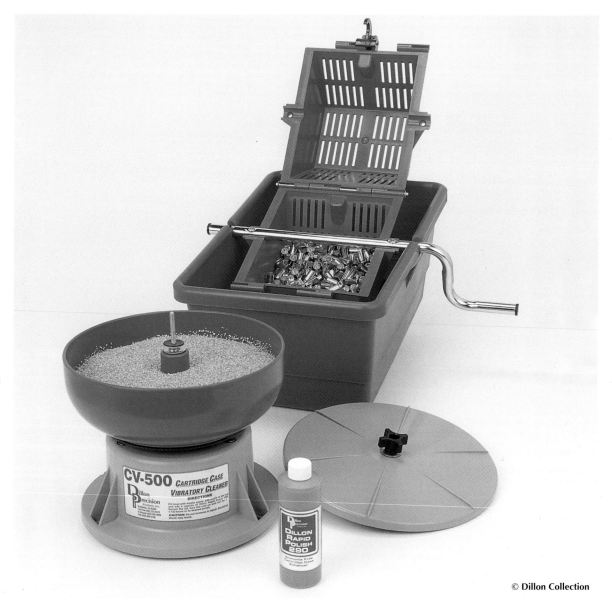

© Dillon Collection

smaller caliber cases) inside of a case, blown-out primer pockets and deformed case rims.

A problem to be aware of when dealing with the older rifle calibers (.25-20, .32-20, .38-40 and

Pictured above are a few examples of the many products Dillon Precision offers for case preparation – shown here are Dillon's CV-500 vibratory case cleaner, CM-500 case/media separator, and Rapid Polish 290 brass polish.

© Dillon Collection

oversize chamber. However, this renders the brass susceptible to deforming with very little encouragement.

Once the brass has been examined and the damaged cases culled, appropriate bullets and powders need to be selected. For use in lever-action rifles, flat nosed bullets are recommended, to reduce the risk of recoil setting off cartridges in the magazine. A rounded shoulder on the bullet is desirable for both rifle and pistol reloading, as it feeds easier into the chamber without the chance of hanging up.

Special Notice Regarding The Toggle-Action Type Firearms
(Henry, 1866, 1873 Winchester Rifles)

The overall cartridge length for loaded ammunition to be used in the toggle-action, vertical-lifter type firearms is very critical. These guns do not have a cartridge cutoff in the magazine. Therefore, if the round is too short, the base of the next round in the magazine will also protrude into the lifter, locking it up. If the round is too long, it won't clear the magazine tube, and again will lock up the lifter. The best way to prevent this from happening is to use a bullet designed for use in this type of firearm. A properly designed lead bullet will have the crimping groove positioned to give a correct overall cartridge length.

A wide variety of powders are available for reloading pistol type ammunition. Check a quality reloading manual for powder suggestions. The Lyman Reloading Manual is probably the single best source for cast-bullet loading data. Most cowboy shooters use fast-burning powders, as they require less powder per shot, and tend to be cleaner burning. A drawback to these powders is

that they only fill a very small portion of the case volume. This can cause two problems. First, because of the volume of the case, it is possible to fit a double charge of powder into a case and not

© Dillon Collection

.44-40) is that the brass for these calibers is very thin and very soft. The reason for this is so that upon firing, the case will expand to give a proper gas seal for even the most worn and/or

Dillon Precision manufactures several different loaders, shown here are the Square Deal "B" (left) and the RL 550B (right). Pictured with optional accessories.

Honest, he's not shooting the bartender; however, the tone-deaf piano player is in deep adobe! Cartoonish caricatures help brighten up a stage, and keep competitors from taking themselves too seriously.

Large caliber single-shot rifles and double-barrel shotguns are used in Plainsman events.

notice it. Depending on the caliber, powder and charge, and bullet weight, this may or may not cause the firearm to blow up. Either way this is something to be avoided. Fortunately, modern progressive reloading equipment makes this difficult to do.

The other problem involves putting an insufficient quantity of powder into a given case, setting up the circumstances for what is called a detonation. This happens irregularly in small arms, but is well documented in artillery. During a det-onation, all of the powder burns at once, instead of burning progressively. When this happens in a single-action revolver, for example, the top strap will usually detach from the rear of the frame, and the top half of the cylinder will disappear. A double charge, if it does any damage at all, may rupture one chamber in a cylinder and possibly bulge the top strap slightly.

A well known gun writer blew up a first generation Colt SAA in .45 caliber, using what would normally be a safe load of Red Dot, but with a lighter bullet seated farther out than intended. He then installed another cylinder, deliberately loaded a double charge of powder, and proceeded to shoot it through the topstrap-free pistol without mishap, proving empirically that the explosion was not due to an unintentional double charge in a cartridge.

Now we are ready to reload ammunition. For loading handgun ammo, we are going to use the Square Deal B (although the sequence is similar on any progressive reloader.) The first station on the loader will resize and deprime the case on the downstroke of the handle. If you are using new primed brass, be sure to remove the decapping assembly first so that you don't inadvertently remove the live primers. After the case is resized and deprimed, you lift up on the handle and push forward on it to seat the new primer. The next downstoke of the handle will dispense a charge of powder and slightly flare the mouth of the case to make it easier to start seating the bullet. When using new brass, it will normally require extra effort to lift up on the handle and withdraw the charged case from the funnel. This occurs because new brass is rough internally from the impact extrusion manufacturing process. Once the cases have been fired a couple of times, this phenomena will cease.

Station three is the bullet seating station. You set the bullet on the case, and pull the handle down to press the bullet into the case. The machine will include a variety of bullet seating stems, so choose the one that most closely matches the profile of the bullet.

Station four is a separate crimping station. Most loads for cowboy shooting generate little recoil, so a heavy crimp is not necessary. For lever-action rifles, be sure to use enough crimp to prevent the bullet from being pushed back into the case during recoil. Test this by putting the nose of the bullet down on your bench and pressing on the back of the case. The bullet should not push back into the case. Finally, the loaded round is ejected into a collecting bin for final inspection of the loaded rounds.

Loading rifle ammunition is very similar to loading handgun ammunition, except that a couple of extra steps are necessary. The RL 550B is the machine we will rely on for rifle reloading (though again the process is similar on other progressive reloaders). First, rifle brass (and any bottlenecked cases) MUST be lubricated prior to resizing. Otherwise, enough friction results that the rim will rip from the case and the case will be stuck in the sizing die. Dillon Precision makes a non-aerosol spray case lubricant that's easy to apply. Just lay the cleaned brass flat in a cookie sheet, spray a light coat of lube on the brass, agitate the tray to roll the cases around, spray another coat, and wait five minutes for the carrier to evaporate. The first station will resize and deprime on the downstroke of the handle, and reprime at the end of the upstroke. Then manually advance the shellplate to the powder drop station. Pulling the handle down with a case in station two actuates the powder measure, and for some calibers also flares the case mouth. Station three seats the bullet, and station four crimps the cartridge. Then the completed cartridge is then ejected into a catchbin.

LOADING BLACK POWDER CARTRIDGES AND/OR PERCUSSION REVOLVERS

Loading black powder, either in a cartridge or a percussion revolver, doesn't attract much of a following among Cowboy Action Shooters, but it does warrant some special mention. For loading black powder cartridges, some special instructions are necessary in addition to the standard loading process.

First and foremost, DO NOT USE BLACK POWDER IN A POWDER MEASURE! All black powder should be measured separately and then poured through a drop tube into the case. This greatly reduces the risk of igniting the powder,

and compacts it in the case, resulting in more consistent ignition. Next, always use magnum primers with black powder. This gives better ignition and tighter, rounder groups. A target group strung vertically is a good indicator of poor ignition. Use enough powder to allow for 1/8-inch of compression when the bullet is seated. Also, a soft bullet lube, such as SPG brand, is preferred with black powder, as it helps keep the powder residue soft. This gives improved accuracy and more shots fired between cleanings.

Some black powder substitutes are SASS legal. Most cowboy shooters who participate in a Black Powder class do so out of a desire to experience shooting the same way the Westerners used to; smoke, fouling and all. However, some modern cowpokes would rather replace these side effects with special effects. Pyrodex was the first black powder substitute generally available. It still smoked, but it lacked the acrid odor and did not leave the hard, chunky residue of black powder. However, the residue it did leave behind was very hydroscopic. While not actually corrosive, the residue attracted moisture much faster than black powder residue. Cleaning after shooting Pyrodex was much easier, but promptness was essential to prevent oxidation damage.

Black Canyon Powder is a newly approved black powder substitute. While it smokes, it has no odor, leaves virtually no residue, and is casual about cleaning. The drawback to Black Canyon Powder is that at this time it is only available in one grade, extra-coarse. It is too chunky to dispense through most flasks, forcing the user to deal with the original container. Another minor

This well dressed gentleman stands "on deck," ready to take his turn. Attention to one's place in line assures smooth and efficient progress of a posse through a course of fire, with only a few minutes required to load, stand by, shoot, and unload.

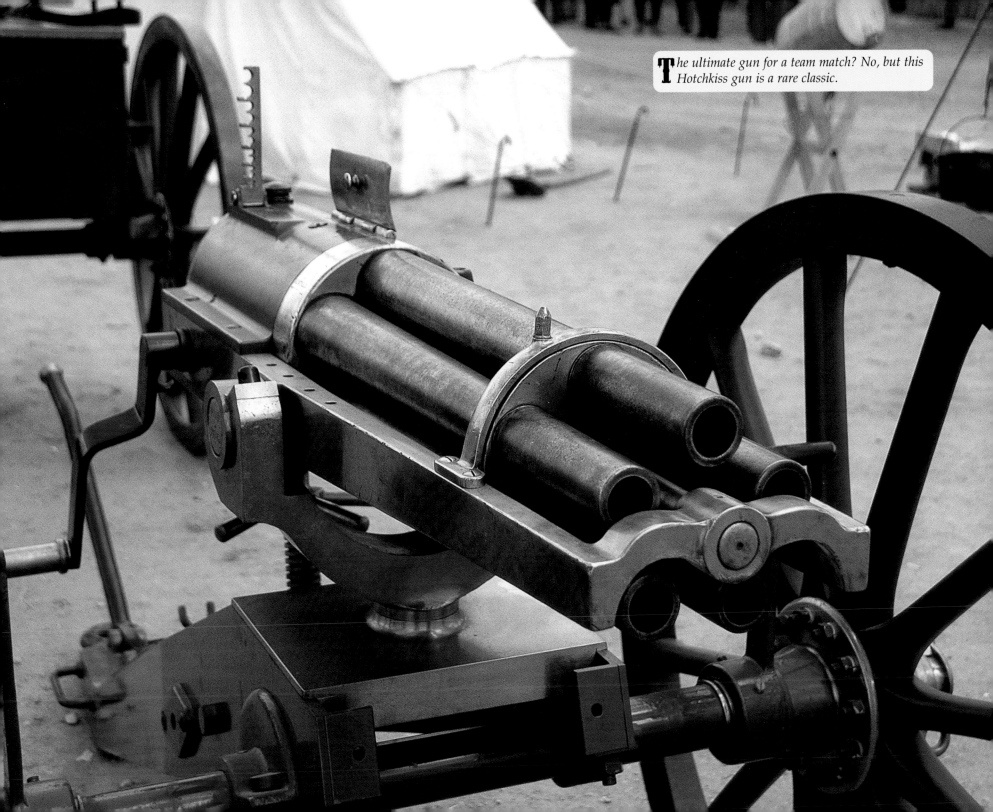

The ultimate gun for a team match? No, but this Hotchkiss gun is a rare classic.

drawback to Black Canyon Powder is that it is approximately 20 percent weaker volume for volume than black powder. While this disqualifies Black Canyon Powder for use in Black Powder Silhouette, it does not preclude its use for any aspect of Cowboy Action Shooting.

Loading percussion revolvers requires patience and a tolerance for mechanisms. Keep in mind that the original users of these firearms carried a brace of them for a very good reason; their reliability is less than that of a cartridge gun. Most competitors who use percussion revolvers are already aware of their idiosyncrasies: percussion caps can split apart upon ignition and bind the cylinder; black powder fouling will bind up the cylinder pin so that the cylinder won't turn; the rammer will unlock due to recoil and lock up the cylinder; most guns have tiny original-style sights and are zeroed at 75 yards. In spite of this, "The Plainsman" side event has become popular at most major Cowboy Action Shooting events, and the "Frontiersman Class" for main-match shooting received final SASS approval in 1996.

Either FFg or FFFg can be used in percussion revolvers. Personally, I've experienced tighter groups and a more useful point of impact with FFg powder; 15 grains for .36 caliber, and 28 grains for .44 caliber. This load is very low in recoil as well. For round balls, the soft swaged round balls as sold by Speer work best. Usual diameters are .375" for .36 caliber and .451" for .44 caliber, but be sure that the bullet is a press-fit into the chambers. A small ribbon of lead should be cut from ball as it's seated. This press-fit is very important, as it seals off the powder behind the ball from the flash of an adjacent chamber

A well-stocked gun cart demonstrates the variety of hardware common to Cowboy Action Shooting.

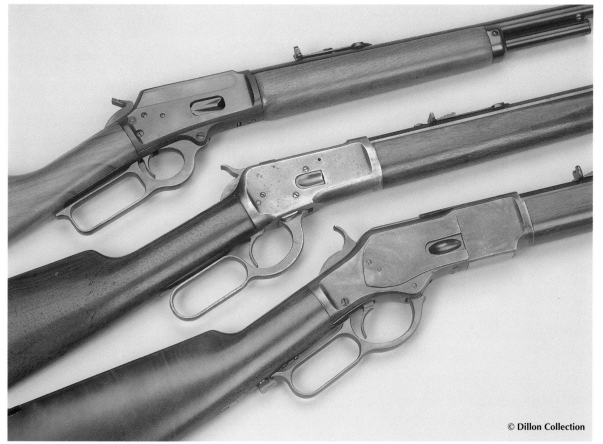

© Dillon Collection

prevent them from falling off. When using too-small caps, they must be forced onto the nipple, or unreliable ignition will occur. Some cowboy gunsmiths offer action work on percussion revolvers that includes reworking the nipples for a better fit with CCI and Remington percussion caps. Otherwise, a poor cap fit is just another part of the percussion experience.

going off. When a failure to seal the powder from an adjacent discharge occurs, it is called a "chain fire," which is spectacular to watch from a safe distance, but can be hard on the shooter. Fortunately, the firearm seldom comes to any lasting damage from this event.

To further help seal off the powder, several methods are available. Originally, grease was

Representative lever-action rifles in cowboy pistol calibers include modern Marlins, original Winchester 92s, and replica Winchester 73s.

smeared over the top of the ball and chamber to seal it. The drawbacks to using grease are that it is messy to work with, and once one shot is fired, the grease over the remaining chambers melts all over. However, the grease does help to keep the fouling soft. A modern and tidier substitute for grease is the Ox Yoke Originals "Wonder Wad," a chamber-diameter treated felt wad that sandwiches between the powder and the ball to prevent flashthrough.

Finally, percussion caps come in two sizes, too small and too large. Most people buy them too large, and have to pinch them in order to

HOOT GIBSON

By age 16, Hoot Gibson was a rodeo cowboy, and he won the "World's All Around Champion Cowboy" title at age 20. In 1912 he started working in films as a stuntman, often doubling for Harry Carey. He was in 114 films during his career, and produced six more.

Edmund Richard "Hoot" Gibson
August 6, 1892 – August 23, 1962

CHAPTER NINE

SACRED COW HIDE

The general preference among Cowboy Action Shooters for authentic firearms and techniques has also brought about new demand for authentic leather gear. Most cowboy shooters prefer their gunleather to follow the historically correct designs, as opposed to the Hollywood buscadero and quick-draw rigs. Very few of the latter are seen on the firing line.

Historically, western holster design generally proceeded as follows. Keep in mind that holster use for different styles overlapped heavily, and varied with the spread of civilization and the geographical area. Immediately following the Civil War, many military holsters were modified for civilian use. Flaps were cut off, belt loops were reversed for a butt rearward carry, and generally reworked to better meet civilian requirements. The civilian holsters of the era, known as the "Slim Jim" and the "California" styles, were long, narrow and closely patterned after lines of the percussion revolvers they held. During the early 1870s, the "Texas" or "Mexican" style of single-loop holster was developing. With this hol-

ster, instead of a sewn belt loop, a fender is cut out of the same piece of leather as the holster, folded behind the holster, slotted and the holster inserted through the loop. By the mid-1870s, the rear fender grew longer and another slot was added. This double loop design soon became the most popular holster style in the Southwest.

In the northern plains of Wyoming, Montana, and the Dakotas, a variation of the loop holster developed in the 1880-1890 period. The "Montana" style of holster had a single wide loop, but instead of being cut from the fender, the loop is a separate piece of leather that is riveted to the fender. By the turn of the century, these two styles, the double drop loop and the "Montana" style, dominated holster design.

Shoulder holsters, largely a western creation, started to appear around 1880. These were the pouch type, like a "Slim Jim" holster sewn to a strap that ran around the shoulder and neck. The spring type, or skeleton shoulder holster appeared in the mid-1890s.

Cartridge belts followed a similar line of

development. In the post-Civil War period, many military and civilian trouser belts had cartridge loops sewn on. These early belts typically were narrow (1-1/4 – 1-1/2-inch wide) and thin. By the mid 1870s, belts grew wider to better support the additional weight, but were still single thickness. Soon after, the belt was made twice as wide, folded and the seam sewn together, creating a tunnel wide enough to fit a silver dollar or a $20 gold piece into, for safekeeping. Thus the money belt was developed.

Shotgun shells historically were carried in a web waist belt, using sewn-on loops to hold the shells. There is no historical evidence for use of a wrist cuff with shot-shell loops, or for a lace-on cheekpiece incorporating shot-shell loops. Most major matches do not allow the use of cuff-type shell holders, either prohibiting them completely or else using stage design to force everyone to retrieve their shotgun shells from the same pre-staged location. Most cowboy shooters use either a belt slide shot shell holder or a web waist belt to carry shot shells. The belt slide is the more

convenient method, but the web belt, if worn above the pistol belt, is faster. This is because it holds the ammunition at about the same height as the receiver of a dismounted shotgun. The shells are closer to the breech of the gun and require less hand movement for a reload.

Rifle ammunition historically has been carried in a variety of ways. In the Post-Civil War period, rifle ammo was carried in a cartridge box. This is a leftover from the era of paper cartridges that stayed with the military until the 1880s. Civilians had changed to leather cartridge belts for rifle ammunition by the early 1870s, but the military postponed this change until adopting the web Prairie Belt in 1879. The military continued to use web belts, with either sewn or woven loops, until advent of the 1903 Springfield. South of the border, the "bandolier," a cartridge belt designed to go over one shoulder and under the other arm, became popular in the 1890s with adoption of the Spanish Mauser bolt-action rifle.

Cowboy Action Shooting stages requiring a rifle reload are uncommon, but expect to encounter one or two at any major match. For this limited use, most shooters rely on a vest pocket for reloads. The problem with bandoliers is that as you use up ammunition, they have a tendency to try to shift position around you. As with shot shells, a web cartridge belt is the best way to carry extra rifle rounds, as it positions the ammunition higher on the body so they are about the same level as the dismounted rifle, for quicker reloading.

During the early 1870s, the "Texas" or "Mexican" style of single-loop holster was developing. By the mid-1870s, the rear fender grew longer and another slot was added. This double loop design soon became the most popular holster style in the Southwest.

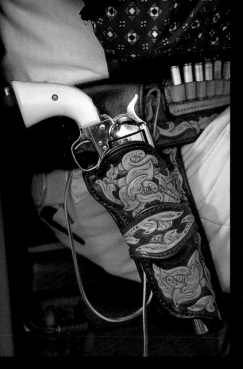

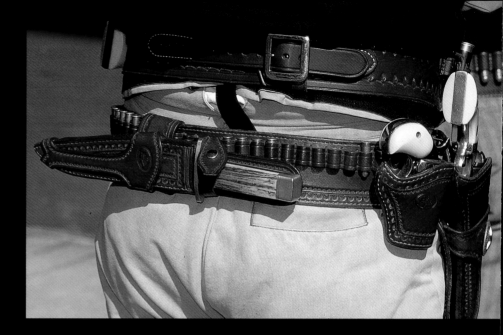

Leather holsters and accessories come in a wide
variety of colors and designs (to say the least).
Holsters, belts, boots, etc. can be magnificently
elaborate or beautifully basic.

SAN PEDRO SADDLERY CO.

The San Pedro Saddlery Co. line of western gunleather is sold by dealers. This gear is all designed from original gunleather of the 1870s-1890s period. It is high quality production leather, with holsters made of the best quality 9-10 oz. full grain cowhide, lined with 2 oz. pigskin. Pigskin lining is preferred over suede, as the pores are smaller, to retain less grit. Belts are made of 10-11 oz. cowhide. All leather products are machine stitched with nylon thread.

San Pedro Saddlery has a limited lifetime guarantee. Not covered is damage due to abuse, neglect or cattle stampede (unless yer story's real good).

For the interest of those who worry about total authenticity, the first mechanical harness stitcher was made by the Pearson Company in 1863.

STEWART SADDLERY

Jack Stewart of Stewart Saddlery takes a different approach to his gunleather. Jack was forced into leathersmithing when he got involved in Civil War re-enacting. At that time, the sources for quality cartridge boxes, knapsacks, etc. were almost nonexistent, so he started to make his own. Eventually he was hired to work at The Sharlot Hall Museum in Prescott, Arizona – an Arizona Historical Society Museum. There he used Smithsonian Institute techniques to catalog, repair and restore original articles. While there, he learned a fundamental difference between military and civilian gear. Military equipment is functional, but civilian gear is beautiful. Jack decided he enjoyed working with leather so much that he should try to make a career of it.

Stewart Saddlery specializes in custom sad-

In the post-Civil War period, many military and civilian trouser belts had cartridge loops sewn on – some more than others.

© Dillon Collection

dles and gunleather, all of original vintage. Jack enjoys completely recreating the old equipment. All leather is hand-cut and hand-stitched. He even goes so far as to have custom rivets made to duplicate originals. Jack feels that this makes a superior product, and that it upholds the integrity of the craft. His goal is to offer a product that is the equal of an original in every way, except that it is brand new. Most recently, Jack's work was prominently featured in the book *Packin' Iron* by Richard Rattenbury. Frequently customers order leather by page number. Jack also does work for many museums, recreating original saddles, chaps and holsters that are too damaged or deteriorated to restore.

KICKING MULE OUTFITTERS

Another custom leathersmith is Garrett Roberts of Kicking Mule Outfitters. Roberts makes hand-tooled reproductions of authentic western holsters and gunbelts, some of which have been used in motion pictures and television productions.

For care and cleaning of gunleather, what you should not do is far more important than what you should do. For cleaning gunleather, a good grade of bar type glycerin saddle soap is best. Most new leather will not require oiling, unless exposed to inclement weather. If you feel a need to oil any gunleather, most leathersmiths recommend using olive oil or a 50/50 mixture of pure neatsfoot oil (produced only from crushed beef hooves – beware of imitations) and olive oil. Regular neatsfoot oil has two problems. First, it is affected by temperature. As the leather gets hot, it sweats out the oil. As it cools, it absorbs the oil.

A basket-weave pattern and decorative studs provide an eye-catching combination. Military equipment is functional, but civilian gear is beautiful.

When drying a wet holster, be sure not to crush it. Instead, as it dries, mold it back into a pistol-friendly shape. Then oil the holster with either of the above-mentioned oils. Put it on by hand and rub it in. Wipe off any excess oil that the leather doesn't absorb.

It is not recommended to keep brass cartridges stored in leather loops. Over time, the tannic acids in the leather will react with the brass, leaving a nasty green sticky coating on the

Olive oil is much more consistent. The other problem is that some neatsfoot oils also contain dyes. So, as you wear your gunbelt, your body heats the leather. Then, when you take your belt off, you have this oily brown stain wrapped around your clothing.

If your gunleather has gotten wet, first wipe all of the water off using a plain towel. Next, let the leather dry at room temperature. Keep wet leather away from any heat source!

brass wherever it contacted the leather, called verdigris. Depending on how thoroughly the leather was rinsed off after the tanning process, this verdigris buildup may take from two weeks to several months to occur.

Leather holsters, belts, boots, pouches, cartridge belts, coats, cuffs, gloves, hat bands, suspenders, shoes, vests, jeez – what **can't** you make out of leather?

PAYING A DEBT

HANDSOME VALENTINE NEVER WELSHES ON A GAMBLING DEBT, NO MATTER THE COST IN DOLLARS OR HUMILITY. OF COURSE MOST COWBOY SHOOTERS AREN'T GOING TO GAMBLE THEIR LOCKS ON THEIR SHOOTING ABILITY AGAINST THE LIKES OF COLUMBUS D. SHANNON.

CHAPTER TEN

SHOOTING EVENTS "ON THE SIDE"

Side events at cowboy matches are growing both in popularity and variety. These lesser stages allow participation in more specialized types of shooting, that, although they may be significant, either do not appeal to all Cowboy Action shooters, or require more exotic types of firearms and equipment. These side matches include various long-range rifle competitions, stages for non-standard pistols such as derringers or pocket guns, and "Plainsman" events, requiring cap and ball revolvers and single-shot rifles using black powder ammunition. In addition to allowing shooters to pursue some of the more specialized forms of shooting, these side events also provide a greatly needed excuse to buy more guns!

LONG-RANGE SHOOTING EVENTS

Long-range shooting events are typically broken into three classifications; pistol-caliber repeating rifle, rifle-caliber repeating rifle and single-shot rifle. Regardless of classification, the number of hits is the determinant of winners; time is only used to break ties.

For **Pistol-Caliber Long-Range Repeating Rifle Class**, shooters can use the same rifle they use in the main stages. Of late, shooter preferences for a specialized rifle for this class lean towards an 1892 Winchester chambered for .25-20 or .32-20. This rifle has a long sight radius, is muzzle heavy for superior offhand shooting characteristics, and in these calibers has a relatively flat trajectory.

The **Rifle-Caliber Long-Range Repeating Rifle Class** requires a large-caliber lever or pump-action exposed hammer rifle. Cartridges must have been designed prior to 1900, and ammunition must use a lead bullet. The .25-35 Winchester is the smallest caliber legal for this class, but .30 WCF and .45-70 are the most popular cartridges. Current-production Winchester, Marlin and Browning lever-action rifles are the most common, but many original big bore rifles can still be seen on the firing line. Of the Winchesters, the models of 1876, 1886, 1894 and 1895 are acceptable, as are their Browning copies. Marlin Models of 1881, 1893 and 1895, and the

current 336 series comply as well. Occasionally, a Whitney-Kennedy, Ballard or a Spencer converted to .50 Centerfire will be seen.

The **Single-Shot Long-Range Rifle Class** is meant to emulate the long distance shooting of the hide-hunting era of the 1870s and early 1880s. Targets may be as close as 200 yards or as distant as 900-1000 yards, but the firearms used are the same. Because of their historical significance, Sharps rifles are among the most popular for this event. The 1874 model, the archetypical "Buffalo Gun," is recreated by Shiloh Rifle Manufacturing and by the Italian armsmaker, Pedersoli. The Italian version has an attorney-designed wing safety on the firing pin, but is a well-made and very accurate firearm. It is also reasonably priced and readily available. The Pedersoli Sharps is imported by Armsport, Navy Arms and EMF.

The Shiloh Sharps is manufactured in Big Timber, Montana, and should qualify as a work of art. The stock fit is so tight that the wood looks like it was grown onto the action. Everything about these arms is nothing short of perfect. They

1000. Thus, the wait for a Shiloh Sharps is about four years. What many shooters do is acquire any Sharps to shoot for now, then place an order for the Sharps of their dreams.

Another popular rifle for long-range single-shot matches is the Browning 1885 High Wall. It was introduced too late for the hide hunting period, but remained in production until 1920. The High Wall is faster to operate than most of the other single-shots of the era, because opening the action cocks the hammer as well as ejecting the fired case. Most other single-shots require cocking the hammer as an additional step, separate from opening the action.

Other popular single shots include Remington rolling block rifles (both original Remingtons and Pedersoli-manufactured reproductions via Navy Arms), Springfield trapdoor rifles and carbines, and a myriad of other lesser-known original single-shot firearms of the pre-1900 era.

Tang rear sights are allowed on rifles in all SASS shooting. They are helpful in the main match, but they are essential for long-range work. For the Sharps, Remingtons and High Walls, there are several manufacturers of elaborate adjustable front and rear sights, mostly at very high prices. For the lever-action rifles, Lyman has recently reintroduced their No. 2 Tang sight for Winchester and Marlin firearms.

Another group of side matches revolve around the other types of historically significant pistols used in the West, such as derringers, pocket pistols and double-action revolvers. These firearms seldom see use in main stages because they either require special handling skills or are uncompetitive due to size or action type.

THE DERRINGER SIDE EVENT

The "derringer," often used in the Old West by gamblers, prostitutes, badmen and as a hide-

shoot very well, they are available in almost any of the original chamberings, and they are made of the highest quality materials. However, like any custom or semi-custom firearm, they are not inexpensive. But more awe-inspiring is the fact that demand exceeds supply by a factor of about

Above – Kodiak with his Sharps rifle, outfitted with a vernier tang sight.

Right – Winter Range 1999 Quigley Match winner Gary "Mogollon Munk" Kieft.

Facing Page – Sharps, Remington Rolling Block, Winchester High Wall, or Trapdoor Springfield – no one rifle dominates the long-range rifle side events.

out piece for lawmen, requires shooters to be very familiar with the pistol for safe handling. Thus, its use in cowboy shooting is usually restricted to side matches.

Rarely do both barrels of a derringer print anywhere near each other except at the closest ranges. Therefore, most derringer matches are shot at seven yards or less. The greatest hazard potential of shooting a derringer is during the reloading process. While reloading, it is very easy to point the gun at oneself due to the short length of the barrels.

The safest way to reload a derringer is to hold the barrel assembly in one hand, pointing safely downrange, release the barrel catch, and pivot the gripframe assembly out of the way while ejecting and reloading.

American Derringer Corporation and Davis Industries are the only current manufacturers of traditional derringers. American Derringer offers an all-stainless steel product, available in a multitude of calibers. Keep in mind that a derringer doesn't offer much in the way of a gripping surface, and any of the large-caliber offerings generate a bunch of recoil, which slows down any second shots, and can be pretty painful as well. In derringers, .38 Special is probably the most popular chambering for Cowboy Action Shooting, using either light reloads or .38 Short Colt ammunition.

Davis Industries offers a less expensive variant of the derringer, utilizing alloy castings combined with a steel barrel assembly. Davis derringers are offered in .25 ACP (BLAAH!!!), .32 ACP and .38 Special. Both the American and the Davis offerings have a hammer block safety, which makes the reloading sequence safer (as long as it's used).

Many used derringers can be found, ranging from FIE/EXCAM derringers in .38 Special to a

beautiful A. Uberti model in .45 Colt, with a case-hardened receiver, to the original Remingtons. Navy Arms used to import .41 Rimfire ammunition for use in the Remingtons, but has discontinued carrying it. If you are going to shoot an original Remington, please have it inspected by a qualified gunsmith. The original Remingtons were susceptible to broken hinges, and many were indifferently treated after shooting black powder ammunition.

THE POCKET PISTOL SIDE EVENT

Pocket pistols are another group of historically significant firearms best relegated to side matches. Pocket pistols fall into two categories depending upon the mechanism: single-action or double-action. SASS rules for single-action pocket pistol competition specifically exclude the sher-

iff's model SAAs; therefore no new examples of "single-action pocket pistols" are available. Fortunately, Smith & Wesson alone made over 460,000 examples of single-action pocket pistols in various calibers. Colt, Marlin, and Harrington & Richardson all made thousands more. Navy Arms now imports .32 short and .32 long rimfire ammunition, thus making even more of these pocket guns shootable. Again, before shooting any old, original pistol, have it checked by a competent gunsmith.

Double-action pocket pistols are another class of firearm for which no new versions are avail-

The only three-screw single action left in the line, Ruger's Old Army is a totally "modern" percussion revolver. Originally available only with adjustable sights, Ruger introduced a fixed-sight version specifically for cowboy shooters.

Capt. Chunky, shown here shooting a Shiloh Sharps. Hell no, the old brass scope isn't SASS legal, but it looks really cool and is correct to the period.

WILD BILL ELLIOTT

I grew up in that wonderful time before TV when All Our Heroes Were Cowboys. The week always dragged during the school year until Saturday arrived and we could head to town for the Matinee, which always featured "B" Westerns. There were dozens of great stars, but my favorite was Wild Bill Elliott. Every time Wild Bill said, "I'm a peaceable man," we knew trouble was about to start. Bill packed those twin Peacemakers butt to the front in twin holsters and he had that way of "throwing" the gun forward as he shot that always made it seem a little more dramatic. Whether he portrayed Wild Bill Hickock, or Red Ryder, or himself, it didn't matter. We all knew that Wild Bill was what cowboys were supposed to be.

John Taffin
Field Editor, American Handgunner Magazine

TEX RITTER

Most remembered as a country music recording star, Tex Ritter appeared or starred in 67 films from 1936 to 1961. Tex sang the theme song for the movie classic "High Noon" starring Gary Cooper. Tex REALLY was born in Texas, and most of the characters he portrayed were dubbed "Tex."

Woodward Maurice "Tex" Ritter
January 12, 1905 – January 2, 1974

*I*n addition to allowing shooters to pursue some of the more specialized forms of shooting, side events also provide a greatly needed excuse to buy more guns! Just ask Dillon's Denis "Gatling" Plewniak.

able, but plenty of originals are available. Many thousands of what are now termed "suicide specials" were made, being most notable for their dubious quality, but higher quality, brand-name double-action pocket pistols were made as well. Many Smith & Wessons, Merwin & Hulberts, Iver Johnsons, and Harrington & Richardsons can be found at gun shows or used gun shops. Colt made the famous "Lightning" and "Thunderer" models of 1877 double-action revolvers, respectively chambered for .38 Long Colt and .41 Colt, but these firearms are notoriously cranky and fragile. They have a very intricate trigger mechanism which can easily fail. If you have a properly working example, it should spend most of its time in the gun safe.

Most pocket pistol side matches require five shots at very close range, with possibly a reload thrown in for added fun. Some course designers use alternative targets, like playing cards or poker chips, to give a western flair to the stage, and promote some precision shooting.

THE "ORIGINAL DOUBLE-ACTION REVOLVER" SIDE EVENT

Another side match that is gaining in popularity employs the original large-bore (.38 caliber and up) double-action revolvers. In this category the Smith & Wesson Double-Action Frontier Model; Colt double-action revolvers, the Colt 1877 and 1878; and the Merwin & Hulbert double-action revolvers are the best known examples. This side match allows owners of these historic arms to use them competitively; otherwise

Any six-shot percussion revolver is acceptable for the Plainsman event. This event was introduced at the first Winter Range match in 1992, and quickly became one of the more popular side matches.

Getting ready to go to the line involves careful loading with powder, ball, and percussion caps.

their double-action mechanisms disqualify them from main stage competition. Many of these firearms have unusual (and fragile) mechanisms, and thus require gentle handling. However, if in good condition these guns won't suffer from a limited amount of shooting, and most Cowboy Action shooters would rather clean powder fouling from their guns, rather than just wipe the dust off occasionally.

THE PLAINSMAN SIDE EVENT

The post-Civil War era western expansion is represented by the "Plainsman" side match. Using percussion revolvers, single-shot rifles chambered for a traditional black powder cartridge and double-barrel shotguns, this match is punctuated by the white smoke and sulfur odor of black powder (or its less stimulating imitators). This event was introduced at the first Winter Range match in 1992, and quickly became one of the more popular side matches.

Any six-shot percussion revolver is acceptable for the Plainsman event. Sturm, Ruger & Company, aware of the growing interest in this event, recently introduced a fixed-sight version of their percussion Old Army revolver. Made of modern, heat-treated steel, the Ruger Old Army is the ultimate percussion revolver (especially in stainless steel). However, you do not need a handgun of this quality to compete. Many shooters use the inexpensive brass frame copies of the original Colt and Remington cap and ball revolvers for the Plainsman event, but for a marginal cost difference, one can purchase a steel frame gun and have a much more durable firearm. Of the reproduction percussion revolvers, those made by Uberti are the most authentic, being complete down to the safety pins in the cylinders of the Colt models.

Most of the Colt reproductions tend to shoot high, as the original front sights were regulated for about a 75-yard zero. Most Remington reproductions now have a higher, windage adjustable front sight that will shoot to point of aim at 25 yards. The advantage with the Colt types is that if a percussion cap splits when firing (as they usually do) they are easier to dislodge from the open top frame of the Colt than from the solid frame models.

Rifles suitable for the Long-Range Single-Shot event are equally acceptable for Plainsman, but most long-range shooters are not too excited about cleaning black powder residue out of a $2,500 Sharps. The Handi-Rifle, made by Harrington & Richardson and New England Firearms Company, chambered for .45-70, is an inexpensive and accurate rifle that is very popular for this event. H&R 1871, Inc., has just introduced a limited-edition variation, called "The Buffalo Classic," with a 32-inch barrel, steel buttplate and 19th Century styling. An alternative to this is to use one of the allowable black powder substitutes, such as Pyrodex or Black Canyon Powder. The later is a non-corrosive, odor-free and residue-free propellant rapidly gaining in popularity. In 1995, SASS ruled that Black Canyon Powder is an allowable black powder substitute.

For the shotgun requirements of the Plainsman event, any SASS-legal double-barrel shotgun is acceptable. For ease of cleaning, a shotgun with a chrome lined barrel is preferable. But Plainsman does offer the opportunity to use the Damascus-barreled shotguns that otherwise can't be safely fired with smokeless loads.

Left – Nine iron to shootin' iron. It's easy to draw comparisons between selecting the right firearm for a stage and selecting the proper club for a golf shot.

Facing Page – Any combination of targets and props can be used to challenge a shooter's skill. To make matters worse, a competitor can be required to shoot "weak" hand only.

CHAPTER ELEVEN
WITH A HORSE, OF COURSE

One of the most spectacular events both to watch and to enter is the mounted shooting event. Cowboy Mounted Shooting is the first shooting sport since the Wild West Shows with across-the-board spectator appeal. Mounted shooting events are now held at rodeos, state fairs and Old West festivals. Mounted shooting is beneficial to the whole sport of Cowboy Action Shooting as it exposes many non-shooters to firearms sports.

The mounted shooting event was developed by Arizonan Jim Rodgers, and introduced at the 1992 Winter Range, as an exhibition to entertain competitors while scores were being tabulated. From this beginning, mounted shooting has grown into a highly specialized event requiring a talented rider and a tolerant horse, and attracts about 10 percent of the total participants in Cowboy Action Shooting. Rapid growth in mounted shooting led to the creation of the Cowboy Mounted Shooting Association (CMSA). CMSA was established to promote the safe production of mounted shooting events, and has established a series of regional events leading up to a national championship. CMSA guidelines are a mix between SASS guidelines and those for team roping. CMSA follows SASS guidelines for traditional firearms and clothing, and also requires the use of pre-1900 style saddles and tack. Like team roping, CMSA uses a system of handicapping to level the playing field between competitors of different skill levels.

Due to the uncertainty of mounted shooting, and the presence of spectators, all responsible mounted events fire ONLY blanks when shooting from horseback. Targets are balloons, which are popped using black powder blanks. This reduces the risk of discharging a firearm from the back of an out-of-control horse by an out-of-control rider toward spectators. At a CMSA-administered event, the only blanks allowed to be shot are those provided by CMSA, and are made available only in .45 Colt. These black powder blanks have a load of corncob media to burst balloons. This is safer than the blanks solely using large charges of black powder, as they are much less flammable, and if someone is accidentally hit by a stray piece of corncob, it won't stick to them and cause a burn. These blanks are effective at 18 to 25 feet.

For the mounted shooting event, two handguns are required. If an event includes firing live ammunition, such shooting will be done dismounted, and not with the same guns fired from horseback. Participants may not have any other ammunition on their persons during the event. Additionally, a designated gunhandler loads and unloads all firearms used in a match.

Stage design is carefully controlled so that all shots fired are directed toward the center of the range. Riders negotiate a specific course of travel, engaging targets in given order. Courses of fire are designed to provide maximum enjoyment to both spectators and riders within the strictest of safety considerations. Safety is paramount; safety of the spectators first, safety of the horses second and safety of the competitors third.

The spectator appeal with mounted shooting is very high, but sometimes it can get excessive.

During the Wonder Bread formative period of mounted shooting, horses trained to disregard gunfire were scarce, and somewhat ambivalent in regard to their retention of this training. At a particular Railhead match, Jim Rodgers had just finished an *exhibition* course on the horse, Chapo. After viewing Jim's run, Shaky Jake Johnson, a longtime compadre of Jim's, opted to repeat the course from the back of Jim's mount.

While Chapo could handle one run through the balloon-festooned course, a second journey

---

During the Wonder Bread formative period of mounted shooting, horses trained to disregard gunfire were scarce, and somewhat ambivalent in regard to their retention of this training.

was just too much to ask. Jake did manage to negotiate the course, but Chapo decided that an impromptu rodeo was in order. Chapo did a good imitation of a buckin' bronco, with Jake managing to stay astride. Unable to eject his noisy rider, Chapo then took off at a dead run through the pine forest surrounding the range. In a matter of seconds Chapo and Jake were out of sight. Tensions mounted as speculation ran rife. Did Jake stay mounted? Did Chapo run him into a tree branch or dump him into a rocky ravine? No shots were heard, so it was assumed that Jake was unwilling (or unable) to shoot a borrowed horse.

After about ten minutes had passed, Jake reappeared, on foot, leading a docile-looking

Chapo. It seems that Chapo ran straight through the woods, Jake working hard to stay in the saddle. After racing pell-mell through the trees for a bout a half a mile, Chapo apparently felt he had gotten his point across and came to a gentle stop, allowing Jake to ooze to the ground. With his feet planted on terra firma, Jake felt it was more discretionary to walk Chapo back to the area.

Stage design is carefully controlled so that all shots fired are directed toward the center of the range. Riders negotiate a specific course of travel, engaging targets in given order. Courses of fire are designed to provide maximum enjoyment to both spectators and riders within the strictest of safety considerations.

TOM MIX

Arguably, Tom Mix was the greatest of all the cowboy stars. In terms of the sheer volume of movies he appeared in, his record is unmatched by any other cowboy star – Tom appeared in 302 films! His career fell victim to technology, however, because he was unable to make the transition to talking pictures. It is said that his dentures made it difficult for him to speak his lines clearly. At the height of his career in the 1920s, his salary was $10,000 per week. In light of that, one might say his first film role in the movie "The Cowboy Millionaire" was a self-fulfilling prophecy. According to his publicity, Tom Mix was a Spanish American War veteran and had been a Texas Ranger. Some controversy exists as to the veracity of these claims. However, there is no question that Tom Mix was a veteran actor. He appeared in his first film in 1909, and with a new, better-fitting set of dentures, he was preparing for a big comeback when he was killed in a freak auto accident.

Thomas Hezikiah Mix
January 6, 1880 – October 12, 1940

From its humble beginning, mounted shooting has grown into a highly specialized event requiring a talented rider and a tolerant horse, and attracts about 10 percent of the total participants in Cowboy Action Shooting.

For safety reasons, mounted shooters use only CMSA-supplied black powder blanks loaded to strictly controlled specifications.

CHAPTER TWELVE

HABERDASHERS

The most important thing about Cowboy Action Shooting is to look good, so finding the right clothing is a major consideration. The ruling maxim for the cowboy shooter is that it's not how good you shoot, it's how good you look when you shoot!

SASS guidelines give minimum requirements for clothing. Tennis shoes, ballcaps, and sponsor logos are forbidden. Straw hats, unless of a historically correct nature, are disapproved of, as are short-sleeved shirts. The emphasis on participation, not just on winning, has evolved cowboy shooting to a point where clothing is as important as shooting. The costume contests of the past have become more of a character portrayal event, where a working persona and what type of pocket knife a person carries is what separates winners from the also-rans.

SASS does recognize "silver screen" western costuming, but the great majority of cowboy action shooters are interested in portraying the historical westerner, be it cowboy,

shopkeeper, school marm, dance hall girl, frontier soldier, Indian, etc.

At one time, participants either had to sew their own clothing by modifying new patterns and dissecting original clothing, or else pay for a tailor to recreate period clothing from scratch. One took a lot of time, the other a lot of money.

Today, there are many sources for authentic western attire. High quality factory production clothing has become readily available. A cottage industry has developed around semi-custom men's and women's western clothes, and historically correct patterns for do-it yourselfers are available.

Sculley/Wah-maker is probably the largest manufacturer of authentic western clothing anywhere. (These are the folks who supplied the costumes for Clint Eastwood's Oscar-winning motion picture, "Unforgiven.") Their offerings include, but are not limited to: bib-front shirts, band-collar shirts, round-collar shirts, Paisley print shirts, cowboy vests, dress vests, canvas duckin' pants, corduroy pants, Herringbone

pants, dusters, frock coats, military shirts, vests and coats, and a variety of related accessories, such as suspenders, bandannas and gauntlets. Sculley/Wah-maker also returns a lot to the sport of cowboy shooting. They are the major sponsor for Winter Range and End of Trail.

FOR COWBOY HATS, THERE IS STETSON, CUSTOM-MADE AND EVERYTHING ELSE

In the latter part of the 1860s, a tubercular hat maker named John Stetson headed west to help his consumptive condition. Exposure to the western climate soon led him to believe his Philadelphia Chapeau wasn't up to western requirements; so, from beaver and rabbit fur, using a hatchet, pocket knife and a few other camping tools, Mr. Stetson made a hat he felt was more appropriate for the locale. The primary characteristics of this hat were its high crown and wide brim. Soon after, a wandering cowboy happened upon Mr. Stetson and, after a five dollar transaction, rode off wearing Stetson's creation.

Five dollars for a hat in the late 1860's was a value worth remembering. In 1870, when John Stetson returned to his hattery in Philadelphia, he remembered the cowboy and the hat. He made a few more examples, given the moniker "The Boss of the Plains," and sent them to some western

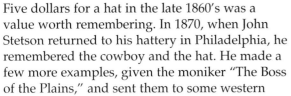

SASS does recognize "silver screen" western costuming, but the great majority of cowboy action shooters are interested in portraying the historical westerner, be it cowboy, shopkeeper, school marm, dance hall girl, frontier soldier, Indian, or even firemen.

merchants. Soon he was inundated with orders. Stetson became THE name in hats. The Texas Rangers adopted them. Annie Oakley, Buffalo Bill, Wild Bill Hickock and Calamity Jane each wore one. Custer died wearing one. By the time of John Stetson's death in 1906, Stetson Hats was producing 4,000,000 per year. Currently, Stetson Hats offers its "Old West Collection," featuring eight primary hat designs. From these, a hat representative of any era can be formed and blocked.

To get a hat of a more personal nature than a Stetson, you have to go to a custom hatter. A cus-

tom hat can be of any style, color, grade of felt and will be fitted to your head. Kevin O'Farrell of O'Farrell hats in Durango, Colorado, and the Az-Tex Hat Company of Phoenix, Arizona, both produce custom cowboy hats of the finest quality, using original 19th century tools and techniques. An instrument called a formillion is placed on your head and adjusted to match its contours, then a card is inserted and punched to preserve the dimensions. Next, the information on the card is transferred to another old machine called a conformeteur, upon which a felt hat is clamped

for final steaming and molding. Upon removal, your custom hat fits you like your head had been training it for years.

The quality of hats is rated in "Xs." Generally speaking, the more Xs, the better the quality. However, there is no standard for X rating. Be sure to talk to your hatter about how much beaver is used in the hat. The more beaver, the better and lighter a hat is (and the more expensive, as well). A 100% beaver felt hat can easily run over $1000!

YOU BET YOUR BOOTS!

Buying boots is similar to buying a hat. There are custom bootmakers, a few appropriate production boot manufacturers and everyone else. If you want a square-toed, one-piece front style of boot, as worn from the 1840s to about 1880, you will be far happier obtaining them from a custom bootmaker. Montana Boot Company offers handmade boots of the classic square toe design, with a pegged sole, hob-nail heels of the various authentic styles and a one-piece front. Custom boots like these require measurements at up to nine different places to ensure a proper fit; otherwise the wearer is doomed to suffer from pain sufficient to ruin any cowboy match.

If you do not want the early one-piece style of boots, then a few of the production makers offer historically correct boots. Olathe Boots has been making cowboy boots for over 100 years. They offer a four-piece boot with a wide rounded toe, a style dating back to the 1880s. The tops can either be flat, commonly referred to as a "stovepipe," or with arched tops and straps or finger holes to

The costume contests of the past have become more of a character portrayal event, where a working persona and what type of pocket knife a person carries is what separates winners from the also-rans.

115

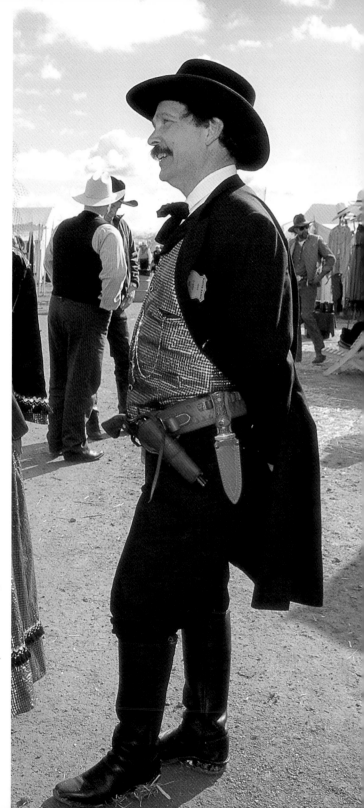

BUCK JONES

DARING ALL FOR HONOR AND FOR LOVE!

Buck JONES

"Sundown Rider"

with BARBARA WEEKS

A COLUMBIA PICTURE

Directed by LAMBERT HILLYER

Cowboy movie hero Buck Jones' last screen role was in part of a series of "Rough Riders" films where he teamed with Tim McCoy and Raymond Hatton. In one film, "Forbidden Trails," Buck narrowly escapes from a house set on fire by the bad guys. Ironically, Buck lost his life in a fire in Boston's Coconut Grove Night Club. The cowboy star died a hero, trying to help people escape the fire.

Charles Frederick Gebhard, aka "Buck Jones"
December 12, 1891 – November 30, 1942

assist pulling the boots on. The arched top started to appear in the 1880s, with the pull straps often being referred to as "mule ears."

Another popular boot which appeared in the 1880s is the lace-up or "packer" boot. This style was popularized by the big game hunters and horse and mule packers of the late 19th century. Olathe Boot offers a quality packer boot, as does White's Handmade Boots of Spokane, Washington.

Wah-maker clothing can be found in specialty shops like Wild West Mercantile, with the full line of Wah-Maker clothing, plus a full line of Olathe boots, Stetson Old West Hats, accessory clothing, historical literature, patterns, gun-leather, reproduction badges, ladies' period shirts, dresses, ladies' dress accessories such as gloves, parasols, purses, etc.

Another specialty shop, River Junction Trade Company, produces smaller quantities of more specialized clothing items like Vaquero pants with leather reinforced seats, Calico trade shirts, other period Indian trade clothing, mackinaw coats, and other esoteric items. River Junction has their own in-house sewing shop, where they produce all of their clothing.

Do-it-yourselfers now have a source for historically correct clothing patterns. Buckaroo Bobbins offers pattern packages for both men's and women's period clothing. This is especially helpful for women's clothing because the Victorian-era styles do not readily lend themselves to factory production techniques.

A final source for cowboy attire that is often overlooked: used clothing shops. Often formal

Facing Page – The lady in red handles her Winchester 97 with aplomb while the hirsute gentleman (right) scans a rifle rack on Sutlers Row.

gowns that have previously been rented can be purchased for ridiculously low prices. With a few minor alterations, you now have a formal Saturday night dress that could have possibly cost ten times as much.

One helpful fashion hint; do not wear a pock-et watch while shooting. If you ever have to bend over during a stage, the chain may wrap itself around the hammer spur on your pistol, causing endless embarrassment. Historically, it did cause one Jim Courtright to pull up short in a shoot-out in Fort Worth, once upon time.

Firing line – Sutlers Row – The Main
Tent! So much to do, so little time!

1847: Loeb (Levi) Strauss and family emigrate from Bavaria to America.

1853: Levi Strauss arrives in San Francisco – sells first "Genes" made of brown tent canvas.

1860: Although still selling brown canvas pants, by this time most of Levi's work clothes were blue. Strauss imported a cotton fabric from Nimes, France. This fabric was available only in indigo blue, and was called "serge de Nimes" or "denim" for short.

1872: Jacob Davis, a tailor from Reno, Nevada, suggests an innovation: Use rivets to strengthen pockets in Levi's pants. Many gold miners car-

FOR THOSE WHO PERSIST IN OSTRACIZING LEVI BRAND JEANS, HERE IS A TIMELINE OUTLINING THE DEVELOPMENT OF LEVIS:

To get a hat of a more personal nature than a Stetson, you have to go to a custom hatter. A custom hat can be of any style, color, grade of felt and will be fitted to your head. Alan Wah (above) admits to owning eight hats! Also shown (center) Ron Bailey and (right) bullet maker Armand Auger.

ried their gold in their pockets and wanted them reinforced.

1873: All Levi's pockets are now reinforced with rivets. Eagle wing pattern now sewn on back pocket in orange thread.

1877: Levi Strauss & Co. commissions a New England factory to manufacture all of its blue denim material.

1886: The two-horse leather patch was added to the back of Levi's pants.

1902: Levi Strauss dies.

The costume portion of the cowboy action shooting sport has plenty of leeway to let anyone assume ANY role they want. It's all in fun.

The whole concept of Cowboy Action Shooting as a competitive sport is to have FUN!

WANTED

FOR REFUSING TO QUIT PLAYING COWBOY

REWARD

AN EXEMPTION FROM GROWING UP
& A ROLLICKING GOOD TIME

CHAPTER THIRTEEN

A CAST OF CHARACTERS, OR... THE USUAL SUSPECTS

DURANGO KID

Larry Cohen, also known as the "Durango Kid," has been a well-known competitor in Cowboy Action Shooting since 1986. Prior to that, Larry was heavily involved in IPSC with California's Southwest Pistol League, and he also ramrodded the Steel Challenge speed shooting competition in Southern California. Larry joined the board of directors of SASS, otherwise known as "The Wild Bunch," in 1987. While there, he introduced his contacts in the shooting industry from the Steel Challenge to Cowboy Action Shooting, thereby greatly improving the random prize program and the level of corporate sponsorship at The End of Trail Cowboy Action Shooting World Championship.

In addition to his administrative talents, Larry is also an accomplished competitor. He won 1991 End of Trail, 1992 Winter Range and placed second at the 1992 End of Trail.

In 1992, Larry closed his veterinary practice in Southern California, retired from "The Wild Bunch" and moved to Durango, Colorado. There, not content to retire, Larry then started and staffed the annual Durango Junction High Country Shootout. Furthermore, Larry developed the posse system for organizing and cycling shooters through the stages of a cowboy match, which has since been adopted for use in most major Cowboy Action Shooting events.

For equipment, he uses the following:

RIFLE: Uberti reproduction 1873 Winchester saddle-ring carbine, chambered for .357 Magnum.

PISTOLS: Pair of Second Generation Colt Single Action Army revolvers, chambered for .45 Colt, with 5-1/2-inch barrels, action jobs performed by Lee's Gunsmithing. Trigger pull weights are two pounds. Gunleather by G. Wm. Davis.

SHOTGUNS: 1897 Winchester pump shotgun, chambered for 12 gauge, 22-inch barrel with modified choke. Original Ithaca side-by-side, chambered for 12 gauge, with 22-inch barrels, open bores.

SIDE MATCH GUNS:

Plainsman event: two Colt Second Generation .36 Navy cap and ball revolvers; 1885 Browning High Wall rifle, chambered for .45-70;

Long range single-shot rifle: Shiloh 1874 Sharps .45 caliber;

Long range repeating rifle: Browning 1886 lever-action, chambered for .45-70;

Derringer: American Firearms Company, chambered for .45 Colt.

CLAUDIA FEATHER

Claudia Ingoglia ("Claudia Feather") came to Cowboy Action Shooting with her husband, Tom ("C. S. Fly"), from eight years of practical pistol shooting. Claudia was first exposed to shooting after moving to Arizona from New Jersey. Once here, her husband enrolled her in a two-day home safety pistol course. This got Claudia hooked on pistol shooting. Finding their way to the Rio Salado Sportsman's Club in Mesa, Claudia and Tom became heavily involved in

both the club and in the practical pistol division, with Claudia maintaining the shooting statistics and publishing the monthly newsletter as well as performing as the club secretary-treasurer.

Tom and Claudia attended their first cowboy match in August 1992. They had so much fun that they started the Cowboy Action Shooting division, known as the Rio Salado Cowboy Action Shooting Society (RSCASS) the next month. Tom is club president and Claudia is secretary-treasurer.

During her shooting tenure, Claudia has amassed her fair share of trophies:

1993 Red Rock, Nevada, event, First place, Women's Class;

1994 Winter Range, First place, Women's Traditional Class;

1994 End of Trail, First place, Women's Traditional Class;

1995 Nevada State event, First place, Women's Class;

1995 Winter Range, Third place, Women's Traditional Class;

1995 End of Trail, Third place, Women's Traditional Class.

Claudia is very competitive by nature, but she enjoys Cowboy Action Shooting as much for its social aspects, the camaraderie, the costuming and the history of the Old West. Her biggest hur-

Facing Page – Denis Plewniak (right – aka "Gatling," of course) pondering the purchase of yet another gun from "Honest Tom Dolbow's Arizona Oceanfront Property and Used Gatling Gun Emporium."

Left – Madison Walker ("Nat Love") – shooter turned historian.

dle was in learning to shoot the rifle and shotgun, but now she enjoys rifle shooting and tolerates the shotgun – recoil is not a factor.

In November 1993, Tom and Claudia opened Wild West Mercantile, a retail shop specializing in clothing, dry goods and accouterments for the cowboy shooter, re-enactor and the western enthusiast. Since opening the store, Claudia's practice time has steadily eroded from twice a week to twice a month – at the matches.

For equipment, she uses the following:

RIFLE: Marlin 1894 Century Limited, chambered for .44-40, with action work by Ogelsby and Ogelsby.

PISTOLS: Pair of Third Generation Colt Single Action Army revolvers, chambered for .38 Special, with 5-1/2-inch barrels, nickel finish and stag grips, with action work by Bob James.

Shotgun: 1897 Winchester pump, chambered for 16 gauge, 20-inch barrel, open bore.

NAT LOVE

Madison Walker ("Nat Love") has been involved in Cowboy Action Shooting since 1992. Madison is involved in many different shooting disciplines, and initially intended only to "taste" cowboy shooting, so he could comment on it in his proactive work on behalf of firearms ownership. However, he found the level of cooperation and camaraderie so high that he felt compelled to get more deeply involved. Additionally, cowboy shooting opened the door for Madison to study the history of black involvement in the West, which is becoming more documented. At the 1995 End Of Trail, Nat Love entered the character portrayal, winning third place.

Cowboy Action Shooting has also led Madison to another hobby, reloading. A need to tailor loads to his specific requirements got him started, and a desire to understand how ammuni-

The scene – The Wild Bunch. The location – Winter Range, 1994. The players – everyone who could field a team. The outcome – a great event!

tion works, the importance of bullet shape, differences between powders, have all forced him to study physics, higher mathematics, metallurgy and related sciences.

In 1995 Madison was elected to the Arizona Territorial Company of Roughriders, the administrative board responsible for the Winter Range National Cowboy Shooting Championship. He holds the position of secretary, setting the agenda and keeping the minutes.

Madison started competing in the modern class, using a Ruger Blackhawk and a Uberti Cattleman, both chambered for .357 Magnum. Peer pressure and his increased interest in the history of the era have pushed him into the Traditional Class.

Nat Love uses the following firearms:

RIFLE: Rossi M-92 carbine, chambered for .357 Magnum

PISTOLS: Pair of Uberti Single Action Army revolvers, chambered for .357 Magnum, one with 4-3/4-inch barrel, the other with 7-1/2-inch barrel. Also a Hawes single-action revolver, chambered for .357 Magnum, with a 5-1/2-inch barrel.

SHOTGUN: IGA double-barrel, chambered for 12 gauge, 20-inch barrels.

CHINA CAMP

Dennis Ming ("China Camp") is the reigning champion of Cowboy Action Shooting. He has won dozens of local and regional matches, won at Winter Range 1993 and 1994, and won End of Trail 1992, 1993, 1994 and 1995. Dennis has a very strong shooting background; he has been at every End of Trail. Other shooting experience

Right – Dennis Ming ("China Camp") is the perennial champion of Cowboy Action Shooting. Pictured here with his wife Jeanie Ming ("Prairie Weet").

127

includes IPSC with the Southwest Pistol League, Bianchi Cup, Steel Challenge, Soldier of Fortune three-gun matches, plus he is a reserve officer with the City of Orange Police Department, an FBI-certified police firearms instructor and a certified instructor for officer survival. In his spare time, Dennis has been a pharmacist for over 26 years.

Above – John Shaw ("Idaho John") Champion of Winter Range '99.

Right – "Doctor George" with equine friend at Winter Range '99.

HOP-A-LONG CASSIDY

CLARENCE E. MULFORD'S
Hop-a-long CASSIDY

with
WILLIAM BOYD
JIMMY ELLISON

PAULA STONE · GEORGE HAYES
KENNETH THOMSON · ROBERT WARWICK

DIRECTED BY HOWARD BRETHERTON
a HARRY SHERMAN Production
a Paramount Release

Usually I went to the movies with my fellow traveler Alfred Haywood. When you finally got out of the movies into darkening streets, the magic lingered. Once, walking home, I said to Alfred, "When Hoppy hits somebody it goes 'thunk!'" Not being a fighter like some kids, but really curious, I whacked Alfred a good one with my fist. "What was that for?" Alfred said, preparing to repay in kind. "Well, I needed to know if it really goes thunk! But it doesn't!" And that was good enough for Alfred. Once he suggested we try the classic leap off a cliff into the saddle like Hoppy did. I held his gray mare's bridle and Alfred leaped. The drop from the roof of the chicken coop was about five feet, and Alfred was obviously in pain, but I took my turn. It was a BAD, BAD idea.

Nyle Leatham
Photography Editor,
American Handgunner Magazine

Dennis is an effective competitive shooter, but this is probably exceeded by his instructive talents. Both his wife Jeannie ("Prairie Weet") and his daughter Jessica ("Sweetwater") are very successful Cowboy Action Shooters.

Dennis reloads his family's ammunition on Dillon equipment and Lee's Gunsmithing handles his action work. China Camp carries his

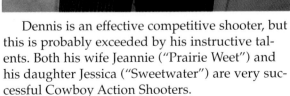

Above left – The ever-popular orator at Winter Range is "Mr. President," actor Mike Cawelti who consistently pleases crowds with his Theodore Roosevelt impersonation. His most frequent advice: "Walk softly, and carry a Winchester!"

Center – Richard Young ("Tequila"), a '98 End of Trail champion, comes off the shooting line at Winter Range '99 demonstrating the safe and

polite way to transport an uncased shotgun: action open, muzzle upright, finger off the trigger.

Safety is a fetish at SASS events, with little tolerance for sloppy gun handling.

Above Right – Machine Gun guru Peter Kokalis ("Poison Pete") donned Rough Rider livery for his Cowboy Action Shooting debut at Winter Range '99.

guns in a custom rig by "Shaky Jake" Johnson.

For equipment, he uses the following:

RIFLE: Navy Arms 92 short rifle, chambered for .357 Magnum.

PISTOLS: Pair of Second Generation Colt Single Action Army revolvers, chambered for .357 Magnum, with 4-3/4-inch barrels and stag grips, and a pair of U.S. Patent Firearms Co.

"China Camp Specials," in .357 Magnum.

SHOTGUNS: IGA double-barrel coach gun, chambered for 12 gauge, with 20-inch barrels, choked for improved cylinder and modified.

1897 Winchester pump, chambered for 12 gauge, with full choke tube installed.

Facing Page – Evil Roy and Wicked Felina passed on their hardcase image to their granddaughter, Holy Terror, but beneath the black hats they're some of the nicest folks you'll find on the range.

Above – 1st Place Posse, Winter Range 1999.

APPENDIX A

THE SASS SHOOTERS HANDBOOK

The Single Action Shooting Society is an international organization created to preserve and promote the fast growing sport of Cowboy Action Shooting. SASS endorses regional matches conducted by affiliated clubs and annually produces End of Trail, the World Championship of Cowboy Action Shooting.

Cowboy Action Shooting is a multifaceted shooting sport in which contestants compete with firearms typical of those used in the taming of the Old West; single-action revolvers, lever-action rifles, and double-barrel, side-by-side, pre-1899 pump- or lever-action shotguns. The shooting competition is staged in a unique, characterized, "Old West" style.

Contestants shoot in several one-, two- or three-gun stages (courses of fire) in which they fire on reactive steel and cardboard silhouette targets. Scoring is based on accuracy and speed.

The truly unique aspect of Cowboy Action Shooting is the requirement placed on authentic period dress. Each participant is required to adopt a shooting alias appropriate to a character or profession of the late 19th century, or a Hollywood western star, and develop a costume accordingly.

Your SASS shooting alias is exclusively yours. In the tradition of the Old West cattle brand registries, SASS prohibits one shooter duplicating another's alias. There is only one Tex, one Kid Curry, one Loophole Pettifogger, etc.

SASS-affiliated clubs are required to respect the sanctity of SASS membership aliases, using them in their articles for publication in *The Cowboy Chronicle* and giving them preference over local club members who may not be SASS members, and who are using a duplicative alias.

American history buffs and serious shooters alike agree that the use of vintage firearms, authentic costuming, unique targets and fast action make Cowboy Action Shooting one of the most interesting of all shooting sports for both spectator and contestant.

This handbook includes the specific rules and regulations and general guidelines adopted by the Single Action Shooting Society. It is the intention and hope of SASS that these requirements will serve to preserve and protect Cowboy Action Shooting from the gimmickry and technical gamesmanship that have had such negative effect on other shooting disciplines. The founders of SASS believe that End of Trail and the associated club and annual matches are as much an opportunity for fun and fellowship as they are shooting competitions.

SPIRIT OF THE GAME: OUR WAY OF PLAYING

As the game of Cowboy Action Shooting has evolved, our competitors have developed and adopted an attitude towards their participation that we call "the spirit of the game." Competing in "the spirit of the game" means that you fully participate in what the competition asks. You do not look for ways to create an advantage out of what is or is not stated as a rule or shooting procedure.

For example, a shooting problem at a club match had the competitor start the stage by knocking a "stick of dynamite" over with a bullwhip. This procedure required swinging the whip across the dynamite stick just a few feet away. It was possible to miss and many did. You had to keep swinging until you got the dynamite.

One shooter, determining that he could shave some time by taking a penalty rather than attempting to knock over the dynamite, simply threw the bullwhip on the ground and went after the targets.

In Cowboy Action Shooting we call this "failure to engage." And it definitely is not in keeping with spirit of the game. Some folks would call "the spirit of the game" nothing more than good sportsmanship. Whatever you call it, if you don't have it, Cowboy Action Shooting is not your game.

EQUIPMENT & SHOOTER CATEGORIES

Originals and reproductions of firearms manufactured during the early to late 1800s by Colt, Winchester, Remington, Smith & Wesson, Marlin, Sharps, Henry, etc., are allowed in SASS competition so long as they are in safe shooting condition.

REVOLVERS

Cowboy Action shooters are divided into four categories: frontier cartridge (black powder), traditional, modern, and duelist. A shooter's classification is determined by the type of "six-gun" he or she uses, the propellant used and the shooting style.

Frontier Black Powder:

Percussion or cartridge, single-action revolvers of original manufacture prior to 1896 or reproductions thereof.

Must be .36 caliber or larger.

Adjustable sights are not allowed.

Black powder, Pyrodex or Black Canyon propellants must be used in all loads. NOTE: Black powder competitors must also use black powder, Pyrodex or Black Canyon propellants in their rifle and shotgun loads in all main matches. Any combination of smokeless and "black" powders (so-called duplex loads) is specifically prohibited.

Competitors choosing to use percussion revolvers may load and cap only five chambers. If a particular stage requires a one shot reload, the sixth chamber may be charged and then capped "on the clock." A complete reload is handled by placing a loaded, uncapped revolver downrange and capping on the clock, or by switching cylinders *a la* Clint Eastwood.

The Ruger Old Army percussion revolver with traditional, non-adjustable sights is permitted in the frontier cartridge class. The same gun in the model having adjustable rear sights must compete in the modern class.

"Black Jack McGinnis," a previous Winter Range champion, stokes up his cap and ball revolvers before sallying forth to tackle the challenges of the ten-stage national title event in 1999.

so long as they are not severely customized so as to constitute a "target" grip. That is, they must be of original shape and scale.

Colored sights and sight inserts are not allowed. Existing sight outlines or inserts must be blackened or removed.

Trigger shoes, compensating ports, counter weights, bull barrels and all other exterior modifications are prohibited. Cosmetic embellishment such as engraving is permitted to the extent that it does not create a competitive advantage. For example, back strap checkering is frowned upon. Engraving your alias on the back strap is permissible.

All handguns other than derringers and small pocket pistols must be carried in a safe holster capable of retaining the firearm throughout a normal range of motion.

Revolver ammunition may not be loaded above a muzzle velocity of 1,000 FPS.

Revolver ammunition may not be jacketed, semi-jacketed or plated. It must be all lead.

Revolver ammunition must be of single projectile design. Duplex, triplex or any such fragmenting bullet is illegal.

RIFLES

Main, Team and Side Matches (Not Long Range or Precision Rifle):

Any lever- or slide-action, tubular-feed, exposed-hammer rifle or carbine.

Centerfire of .25 caliber or larger.

Rifle must be in a "pistol" caliber. (No .30-30, .30-06, .45-70, etc.)

Open iron sights or original style, tang-mounted peep sights are required.

Barrel must be BATF legal, over 16-inches in length.

Traditional:

Single-action cartridge revolver, manufactured prior to 1896, or reproduction thereof.

Must be .32 caliber or larger.

Must have non-adjustable, traditional, notch-style sights.

May use smokeless propellant.

Examples: Colt SAA, Smith & Wesson American, Russian or Schofield, Remington Models 75 or 90, Bisleys, and their reproductions.

The 1999 Winter Range team event afforded shooters the rare opportunity to crank a few rounds from this classic rapid-fire weapon – the Gatling Gun.

Duelist:

Requires a SASS-legal "traditional style" single-action revolver. Black powder or smokeless propellant may be used.

The revolver *must be fired* one-handed, unsupported. (Persons with small hands may use the off hand to cock the gun, but not to support it.)

Modern:

Any single-action cartridge revolver of at least .32 caliber having adjustable sights.

General Restrictions:

Contemporary rubber grips and modern target grips and grip tape are not allowed. Replacement grips of wood, ivory, pearl, stag horn, bone and the like are perfectly acceptable

A well-heeled lady scoops up her Winchester 66 on an urgent errand to beautify Biscuit Flats by depopulating the Winter Range venue in The Great Shootout of 1999.

Rifles with box magazines cannot be used.

Rifle ammunition must be loaded to a muzzle velocity less than 1,400 FPS.

Only lead bullets are allowed. No jacketed, semi-jacketed or plated ammo.

All rifle ammunition must be of single projectile design. No duplex, triplex or other fragmenting loads are allowed.

Long Range (or Precision) Rifle:

Side matches using long range or precision rifle involve slightly different rules. The competitor may use any tubular feed, lever-action or single-shot rifle manufactured before 1896, or any reproduction thereof. All rifles must have external hammers. Sights must be open iron and mounted as on the original rifle or original style, tang-mounted peep sights. Optical and receiver-mounted sights are not allowed.

There are typically four classes in long range or precision rifle:

Single-shot, rifle caliber.

Lever-action, rifle caliber

Single-shot, pistol caliber.

Lever-action, pistol caliber.

Black powder loads can be introduced to any or all of the basic categories at the option of the match director. Each class should compete within itself.

At the discretion of the match director, pre-1900 bolt-action rifles may be allowed as a separate "open" class.

Modern rifles such as the single-shot Ruger Model One, or lever-action Winchester 95 (with box magazine) are not permitted. Reproductions of earlier models such as the Browning 78 are allowed if chambered in a traditional caliber (.45-70, .45-90, etc.) introduced prior to 1896.

Regardless of class or caliber, all ammunition in long range and precision rifle matches must be all lead. No jacketed, semi-jacketed, plated or washed ammo is permitted. Muzzle velocities are restricted only by safety considerations. Extremely high velocities tend to work to the shooter's disadvantage.

SHOTGUNS

Any side-by-side shotgun, typical of the era, *without automatic ejectors,* with or without external hammers, with single or double triggers. Any lever-action shotgun. Any pump shotgun with an exposed hammer (i.e. Winchester Model 97 or Marlin Model 16 except the military configuration of such guns).

No larger bore than 10 gauge and no smaller than 20 gauge.

All shotguns must have a BATF legal barrel length, 18-inches or over in length.

Number 4 lead shot *or smaller* must be used in all events.

Magnum loads are not allowed.

Pump- and lever-action shotguns are allowed to load no more than two rounds at a time in the main matches. In team events, shotguns may be loaded to their maximum magazine capacity.

NOTE: Frontier Cartridge (black powder) shooters must use a side-by-side or lever-action shotgun in their main match stages, but may use any of the above shotguns in team and side matches.

WOMEN, JUNIOR & SENIOR SHOOTERS

Without obligation to do so, any match may define shooting categories for women, junior and senior shooters. When used, such categories should incorporate these standards.

"Juniors" are defined as persons aged 12 through 16. The class may be sub-divided by gender. Caution is urged in allowing competitors under age 12. Parental consent is obviously required for all competitors under 21 years of age.

The women's class may be sub-divided according to the use of "modern" and "traditional" handguns.

SASS defines "seniors" as those competitors who are 65 years of age or greater.

No competitor is compelled to shoot in one of these classes by reason of his or her age or gender. Any woman, junior or senior who wishes to compete under one of the four basic shooter categories may do so. A junior young woman may elect to compete in one of the women's categories. A senior woman may choose to compete in the senior category.

THE PLAINSMAN CATEGORY

This is a special category created specifically to define firearms and shooting style for side matches. The event requires:

Two SASS-legal, percussion (cap & ball) revolvers, fired one handed, unsupported.

A SASS-legal single-shot rifle firing a "traditional black powder cartridge" (e.g. not a .30-30). The cartridges may be either rifle or pistol caliber. The rifle may have spring-actuated ejectors if they are standard for that rifle.

A SASS-legal black powder shotgun (side-by-side, with or without exposed hammers or lever-action).

Only black powder, Pyrodex or Black Canyon powder may be used.

POCKET PISTOLS & DERRINGERS

Pocket pistols and derringers are popular for use in side matches and are frequently introduced as a second or third firearm in main match stages.

A pocket pistol is defined as a small-frame, single- or double-action revolver of a design prior to 1890 and having a barrel of less than four inches in length. It must be of at least .32 caliber. Model "P" Colts are not included in this definition.

A derringer is defined as a breech-loading, small-frame firearm having one-to-four fixed, short barrels. The Remington-style over/under and Sharps four-barrel pepper box are typical. Derringers may be in calibers as small as .22 rimfire.

GENERAL MATCH GUIDELINES

"Pro-Timers" are generally used for timing all SASS events, but stopwatches may be used.

Targets are set at close to medium range.

As a general observation, women require less training to become a better shot…or is it that men have more to unlearn to become a better shot?

Metal and paper targets of generous size are used. Reactive targets such as pepper poppers and falling plates are used when practical to enhance shooter feedback and audience appeal.

NOTE: Cowboy Action Shooting is not intended to be a precision shooting competition. Small targets and long distances tend to take the "action" out of the game.

Both experienced and inexperienced shooters want hits on their targets. Some folks just hit (or miss) a little faster than others. Too many misses, or the perception that the targets are too difficult to hit, discourage folks from continuing to play, especially the less proficient shooters.

Ask any experienced cowboy action shooter and she or he will tell you that *there is no such thing as a target too big or too close to miss!* There are no absolute rules, but we suggest the following distances, by firearm, if using a target approximately 18"x 24":

Derringer	Point Blank to 10" (paper, cardboard or balloons only)
Revolver	20 to 45 feet
Shotgun	25 to 50 feet
Rifle	40 to 150 feet

Decisions of the rangemaster are final.

Ammunition suspected of exceeding the velocity restrictions stated herein may be examined by the rangemaster and he or she shall have final authority in determining the acceptability of any ammunition. Shooters may be held responsible for damage caused to a target because of illegal ammunition.

Firearms of all approved types should be maintained in as original exterior condition as possible. No visible external modifications other than (non-rubber) grips, recoil pads and leather wrapping (e.g. rifle levers) are allowed.

Ammunition required for reloads during the course of any stage must be carried on the shooter's person in a bandolier, belt or pocket. Ammunition may not be carried in the mouth, ears, nose, cleavage or any other bodily orifice.

Bandoliers and cartridge belts must be of traditional design. That is, modern drop pouches, "combat-style" shotgun loops, wrist or forearm bandoliers and such are not in the spirit of the game and are discouraged.

Cartridge loops mounted on a firearm's stock or forearm, while not illegal, are not in the spirit of the game and are discouraged.

SAFETY FIRST, LAST & ALWAYS

Our sport, by its very nature, has the potential to be dangerous and a serious accident could occur. However, the history of SASS-affiliated matches is free of any serious accident.

Every participant in a SASS match is expected to be a safety officer. Each shooter's first responsibility is for his or her own safe conduct, but we expect *all shooters* to remain alert for actions by others who are unsafe.

Any range officer or shooter may confront any participant about an observed unsafe situation and it is expected that the matter will be quickly corrected and not repeated. Any argument by any shooter concerning the correction of a safety related matter can be expected to result in that shooter's ejection from the range.

The following safety guidelines will be adhered to at all times:

Treat and respect every firearm as if it were loaded.

Loaded for bear, this contender levers rifle rounds downrange while sporting a brace of pistols, a substantial Arkansas Toothpick, and a bandolier of scattergun fodder.

All firearms will remain unloaded except while you are under the direct observation of a range officer on the firing line or in the loading area.

All loading and unloading will be conducted only in the designated areas. NOTE: Percussion revolver shooters must exercise extra care to ensure they maintain safe muzzle direction during loading and have fired or cleared all capped chambers prior to leaving the unloading area.

Sixguns are always loaded with only five rounds, the hammer lowered and left resting on the empty chamber.

Long guns will have their actions open, chambers and magazines empty when being carried away from the designated loading/unloading area for each stage.

Long guns will have their actions left open at the conclusion of each shooting string (i.e., whenever the gun leaves the shooter's hands during or at the end of a stage).

Rifles may be "staged" downrange from the shooter with the magazine loaded, action closed, chamber empty.

Shotguns are always "staged" with magazine and chambers empty and are loaded on the clock unless the stage is begun with the shotgun in the shooter's hands.

Handguns are returned to leather (reholstered) at the conclusion of the gun's immediate use unless the shooter has been specifically directed otherwise. For example, when changing from handgun to rifle in a two-gun stage, the handgun will be holstered before the rifle is picked up.

All shooters must demonstrate rudimentary familiarity and proficiency with the firearms being used. SASS matches are not a proper forum in which to learn basic firearms handling.

Alcoholic beverages are prohibited in the range area for all persons: shooters, guests, range officers and others.

No shooters will consume any alcoholic beverage until they have completed all shooting for the day and stored all of their firearms.

No shooters will ingest any substance which may affect their ability to participate with a maximum state of awareness and in a completely safe manner. Both prescription and non-pre-

Tex, a founding member of SASS, conducts research on the long-term effects of black powder smoke on the human body.

scription pharmaceuticals that may cause drowsiness or any other physical or mental impairment must be avoided.

Eye and hearing protection must be worn by all competitors when in the loading area or on the firing line. Such protection is recommended for everyone when in the range area and eye protection is mandatory for spectators when within direct line of sight of steel targets.

SASS-affiliated matches are not fast draw competitions. Any unsafe gun handling in the course of a draw from the holster or any "fanning" will result in the disqualification of the shooter from that stage.

No cocked firearm may ever leave a shooter's hand.

All firearms must remain uncocked whenever the shooter changes shooting location during a stage.

Shooters are expected to perform within their capabilities at all times, with particular concern about controlling the muzzle direction of the firearms being used. A dropped gun will result in the shooter's disqualification from the stage. A "juggled" gun could result in a disqualification. The shooter must never violate the so-called 150/170 degree safety plane.

A shooter may not pick up a dropped gun. The range officer will recover the gun, examine it, clear it and return it to the shooter.

No shooter will have his/her finger on a firearm's trigger until the firearm is pointed safely downrange. Any accidental or premature discharge of any firearm that is determined by the range officer to be unsafe will result in the shooter incurring a timing penalty or disqualification from the stage. A second such incident on the same day may result in the shooter's ejection from the match. A safe practice is to develop the habit of cocking handguns with the "weak" or off

hand after the gun has cleared leather and is pointed safely downrange.

Ammunition dropped by a shooter in the course of reloading any firearm during a stage is considered "dead" and may not be recovered until the shooter completes the course of fire. For example, if a round of shotgun ammo is dropped while reloading, the round must be replaced from the shooter's person or counted as a missed shot. No attempt may be made to pick up the dropped round, as to do so prompts loss of control of muzzle direction.

It is expected that the range officers will be the responsible parties for observing and resolving all safety related matters occurring in the loading, unloading and firing line areas. However, any shooter who observes a safety infraction which is not seen by the range officer(s) may call the infraction to the range officer's attention at which time they will resolve the matter.

Minor safety infractions occurring during a course of fire which do not directly endanger persons will result in a ten (10) second penalty being

Juniors have their own class of competition. Most junior shooters are at least 2nd generation shooters, sometimes 3rd generation, as in the case of "Lightening Bolt," this often gives junior shooters an edge in both safe and proficient gun handling.

added to the shooter's time for that stage. "Minor" safety infractions are occurrences such as an accidental discharge impacting within ten feet, but more than five feet, of the shooter, failure to open a long gun's action at the conclusion of a shooting string, letting the muzzle of a firearm pass through an approximate 150/170 degree arc relative to the shooter and downrange direction or failure to return a handgun to its holster at the conclusion of a shooting string.

Major safety infractions will result in the

Flat Chin Pete runs the timer while China Camp proceeds to turn loaded ammo into dirty, empty brass in record time.

shooter's disqualification from the stage. A second major infraction in the match will result in ejection from the range. "Major" infractions are a dropped gun, an accidental discharge that impacts within five feet of any person, violation of the 150/170 degree safety plane, "sweeping" any person with the muzzle of a firearm and similar acts which have high potential for personal injury.

Only registered competitors may wear firearms.

SCORING

SASS matches are scored based upon elapsed shooting time and added penalty points, generally five seconds, for missed tar-

gets. Each stage is scored individually and, in most club matches, the total combined score for all stages fired is ranked for place of finish, either overall or by class.

At End of Trail, and at the discretion of each affiliated club, rank scoring is used.

In rank scoring each stage is ranked for all competitors' place of finish. At the conclusion of the match, each competitor's rank from each stage is added together and the combined total is then ranked for overall place of finish. For example, if your place of finish in stage one is 23, stage two is 12, stage three is five and stage four is 33, your total rank score is 73. All competitors with lower total rank scores will finish ahead of you.

Rank scoring is recommended when all of the stages in a match are not of approximately the same duration and difficulty.

SELECTING AN ALIAS

Every SASS member is required to select a shooting alias representative of a character or profession from the Old West or the Western film genre. Your alias may not in any way duplicate or easily be confused with any other member's alias. The SASS headquarters is the final arbiter of whether an alias is acceptable or not.

These rules are enforced in accepting a new alias for SASS registry:

It must be "printable" before a wide audience

No duplications are permitted.

If it SOUNDS the same, it is the same.

Adding "too," "II," etc. is not acceptable.

"Ranger" could become "Texas Ranger" but not "The Ranger." "John Henry Chisum" could be modified to "Jack Chisum" but not "John H. Chisum" or "Jon Henry Chisum."

Historical names may not be modified to make them different.

"Wyatt Earp" and "Marshal Wyatt Earp" are considered the same.

The SASS Alias Registry changes daily. Telephone or FAX the SASS office to confirm accurately the availability of your choice of alias.

CLOTHING & ACCOUTERMENTS

Cowboy Action Shooting is a combination of historical re-enactment and Saturday morning at the matinee. Participants may choose the style of costume they wish to wear, but all clothing must be typical of the late 19th century or a "B" Western movie or television series.

SASS puts a great deal of emphasis on costuming because it adds so much to the uniqueness of our game and helps create a festive, informal atmosphere which supports the friendly, fraternal feeling we encourage in our competitors.

All shooters must be in costume and we encourage their invited guests and family also to be costumed. Shooters must remain in costume at all match events: dinners, awards ceremonies, dances, etc.

It is neither difficult nor expensive to assemble a colorful and authentic costume. A little imagination and a dose of creativity can go a long way.

The best way to develop a costume is to first decide on a character or profession you wish to portray. (This is also a good way to decide on your shooting alias, which is mandatory.) SASS shooters have adopted the personas of bankers, blacksmiths, lawmen, gunslingers, railroad engineers, saloon girls, schoolmarms, East Indian British cavalry, U.S. Army cavalry, mountain men, trail cowboys, prairie women, American Indians and silver screen heroes…you name it!

Once you have adopted your character, do a little research. Go to the library and look at historical photographs depicting your character.

Determine the clothing items you need and begin your search.

There are many commercial suppliers of traditional western clothing and accouterments such as River Junction Trade Company, Old West Reproductions, The Old Frontier Clothing Company, Boomtown Mercantile & Trading, G. Wm. Davis & Son, El Paso Saddlery and others too numerous to mention. If your budget allows, these folks and their competitors are great. *The Cowboy Chronicle* usually carries their advertising.

The other way to go is on your own. Visit your neighborhood thrift stores. Look for light weight wool slacks with plaid or vertical stripe patterns or old formals, for example. Men, remove the belt loops from the slacks, add suspender buttons and presto, you have a pair of Old West trousers. Ladies, take the old satin, silk or whatever formal, add a little lace, change a hem line, add a feather boa and a hair comb…*voila*, you're a saloon girl.

Another possibility exists with the commercial costume rental companies. Many of these firms offer a good selection of authentic western wardrobes.

Don't want to get that involved in developing your costume? Well, okay.

Denims of the Wrangler, Levi, and Lee variety are acceptable. Designer jeans (the ones with the colored piping and name embroidered on the pocket) are not allowed.

Contemporary cowboy shirts with snap fronts are okay, but not even very "B" Western. Inexpensive cotton work shirts with button fronts are available at Sears, Roebuck; Montgomery Ward, K-Mart and J.C. Penney stores. These are much more representative of the type of shirt worn in the late 1800s.

If you know a good seamstress or tailor, many patterns for Old West clothing are available. Any large fabric shop will carry cotton goods adaptable to great western wardrobes.

Visit with the other shooters at your local club. They have great ideas about how to assemble a Cowboy Action Shooting wardrobe.

OUTLAWED

Modern shooting gloves.

Short sleeve shirts (roll 'em up if you're hot).

Modern feathered cowboy hats (Shady Bradys). Straw hats of traditional design (Stetson, Bailey, sombreros, etc.) are acceptable.

Designer jeans.

Ball caps.

Tennis, running, jogging, aerobic shoes. (Indian moccasins work well for relaxing after a long day in boots.)

Clothing displaying manufacturers or sponsors badges or logos.

Nylon, plastic, velcro, etc. accouterments.

Mainly, SASS wants participants to be safe, have fun, develop their competitive shooting skills and enjoy the rich traditions of the Old West. We ask that you join us in the friendly spirit of competition and preservation of heritage that we intend.

Single Action Shooting Society
1938 North Batavia Street, Suite M
Orange, CA 92665
(714) 998-1899
FAX: (714) 998-1992
© End of Trail, Inc. 1987, 1989, 1992, 1995
All Rights Reserved,
Used in this book by permission.

APPENDIX B

C.M.S.A. GUIDELINES

The COWBOY MOUNTED SHOOTING ASSOCIATION (CMSA) is the membership organization that promotes and provides rules and guidelines for the equestrian sport of Cowboy Mounted Shooting.

Cowboy Mounted Shooting is a multifaceted equestrian sport in which contestants compete using two single-action revolvers, loaded with blank ammunition specifically manufactured to CMSA standards. Mounted contestants engage 10 reactionary targets while negotiating a specified course of fire on horseback.

A truly unique aspect of our sport is the requirement placed on period clothing, tack and other equipment used in CMSA competitions.

The clothing and equipment used should be typical of that available in the American West during the latter half of the 19th Century.

This handbook contains the specific rules and guidelines adopted by the COWBOY MOUNTED SHOOTING ASSOCIATION, INC.

FIREARMS

Only fixed-sight, single-action revolvers of .45 Colt caliber, designed prior to 1898, or reproductions thereof, will be allowed in CMSA competitions.

Examples: Colt Single Action Army or Bisley Model, Smith & Wesson Schofield, Remington Models 1875 & 1890, their reproductions and Ruger Vaqueros.

All holsters must be of leather construction and must retain the contestants' firearms throughout the strenuous range of motion required in mounted competition. Holsters should conform to the historic Old West design.

Note: Old time high-riding holsters work much better on horseback than the modern Hollywood-type Buscadero rigs.

All firearms must be maintained in the same external condition as originally manufactured from the factory. No visible modifications other than engraving, hammer knurling and/or traditionally shaped custom grips will be allowed. The original external profile must be maintained. All external parts must be of the type manufactured for that particular model of firearm. No part swapping from other models of firearms, i.e., a Bisley hammer cannot be used in a standard Single Action Army Revolver, etc. Hammer turndowns or other "race gun" modifications will not be allowed. Triggers must be operational, "slip hammer" revolvers are unsafe. Each firearm must maintain the looks of a 19th Century revolver, as it would have been used in that era. Birds-head grip single-action revolvers (like the Cimarron Thunderer) are legal if they are offered as standard model from the manufacturer. Sight modifications will be limited to filing the front sight.

SADDLES

Competitors should use "period" saddles of early western design: Sam Stagg-rigged A forks, Hope Trees, American Cavalry Saddles, etc. However, you may still use any saddle of western design as long as it is constructed of traditional materials (i.e., leather) and is in safe condition.

Headstalls, reins, breast collars and tie-downs must be of leather construction. Modern neoprene and fleece-lined cinches, nylon latigos and billets, shin, skid, and bell boots while not encouraged, are acceptable as long as they are of neutral earth tones and do not blatantly change the overall traditional appearance of the competitor's rig. Contestants may use any bit or hackamore to reasonably control their mount as long as it is not overly severe in design.

Traditional leather tack and equipment is more representative of the Old West, and is an enhancement to the sport.

CLOTHING

Cowboy Mounted Shooting is a combination of Wild West show exhibition shooting, cavalry drills, reining competition, barrel racing and historical reenactment. Participants are required to wear authentic clothing typical of the late 19th century. Contestants must dress in period-correct clothing or they will not compete.

The CMSA puts great emphasis on authentic clothing and accouterments. Period dress is one of the most unique aspects of our sport, and a mounted shooter should be the embodiment of the old-time Westerner. Period clothing creates a festive and informal atmosphere, which is characteristic of CMSA events. All competitors must wear period clothing. Short sleeves can be period appropriate; if you are unsure, contact an experienced member. It is also recommended that invited guests and family also wear western clothing. Competitors must remain in period dress at all match events: dinners, award ceremonies, dances, etc. It is neither difficult nor necessarily expensive to assemble a colorful and authentic looking outfit. A little creativity and imagination go a long way. If you are on a tight budget, try visiting thrift stores for long-sleeved cotton shirts and old dress vests. If finances allow, there are numerous manufacturers and vendors of authentic period clothing and equipment for both men and women. Modern clothing like ball caps, T-shirts, tennis shoes and most short-sleeve shirts are not allowed in CMSA competitions.

Promotional logos on tack or clothing will not be allowed in CMSA-sanctioned matches. The only exclusion to this rule shall be for the Makers Mark.

HORSES

CMSA competitions are open to all breeds of horses and mules, registered and unregistered. Riders are expected to compete with mounts that are healthy and in good physical condition. Horses should be introduced and conditioned to the sound of gunfire prior to competing in a CMSA match. A mounted shooting competition is not the appropriate forum to introduce your horse to the sound of gunfire for the first time. New riders and/or mounts must demonstrate that they can safely control or be controlled during the completion of a course of fire prior to

Shooting well is difficult enough without the added challenge of handling a horse at a full run.

entering a competition. Basically, you need a well-trained horse that you can keep under control while negotiating a course of fire with one hand on the reins while shooting with the other.

Introduce your mount to the sound of gunfire gradually from the ground before shooting mounted. Start with a cap pistol or a blackpowder handgun (i.e., replica Colt and Remington revolvers), loaded only with the percussion caps. If your horse handles sound well, then progress to a small charge black powder caliber with 10 grains of FFG grade or .22 blanks and finally the louder .45 Colt blanks used in CMSA competitions. Shooting from the horse should be done at a 90-degree angle from the horse to the target. If you use good common sense and take it slowly, most horses will not react adversely to the sound of gunfire.

Due to the harsher sounds of smokeless gunpowder, you should avoid using blanks loaded with smokeless powder. All mounted shooting ammunition is loaded with black powder or a substitute like Pyrodex.

No more than two riders per CLASS on the same horse with the exception of the Pee Wee class. However, there is no limit on the number of horses that a contestant may use in a CMSA match. In other words, a rider can change horses for each stage. Like roping and team penning events, CMSA matches score contestants, not horses.

No abuse of animals will be allowed. This is a Range Master call. This will be done with a warning first. If disregarded, expulsion from the match will follow.

Even the best trained horses don't always adhere to the training impressed upon them. See Chapter Eleven for the story about Chapo and Jake.

STAGE DESIGN

The "course of fire" or pattern of riding is commonly referred to as a "stage" and should be designed for maximum enjoyment of competitors and spectators, while testing horsemanship and shooting skills. The safety of riders, spectators and horses is a principle concern.

The primary purpose of a stage is to provide a scoring grid that is fair for all contestants. A standard CMSA stage is to have ten targets. A contestant is to engage the course of fire with two single-action revolvers loaded with not more than five approved cartridges. Revolvers are used one at a time. With the first revolver, a contestant engages a random course of fire (the first half of the stage). This random course can be set in any safe manner. Upon completing the random course, the contestant must holster the now empty revolver and draw the second revolver and ride to engage the second half of the stage (called the "run down"). The run down is standardized in all CMSA World Qualifying Matches. The run down is to have five targets to be completed in a fast, forward motion. The final five targets must be staged in such a way that horse and rider are challenged to engage them at a maximum rate of speed, according to their ability. It is specifically not the intention of the CMSA rules to penalize a fast horse and rider.

The Range Master will have the responsibility of making final inspection of course before rider gets their go. Course of fire as set in riders meeting takes precedent over all other possibilities.

- No running starts into the arena
- All riders must start with the gate closed

Barrel will not be closer than 15 feet to the side rails and 25 feet to the end rail and balloons must be a safe distance from the spectators. Try to set course so contestants shoot towards the center of the arena.

After completing the stage, the contestant must immediately report to the armorer and unload both revolvers.

TIMING

Sound activated timers used in conjunction with a stopwatch backup are generally used to time CMSA events. Electronic beam "barrel racing" timers, such as the Pegasus Timer from New Micros, are preferred for larger championship events. In either case, the rider and horse must start the course of fire from behind a predetermined start/finish line.

SCORING

CMSA matches are scored according to elapsed time plus a five (5) second penalty for each target missed. One or more stages (courses of fire) make up a match. The total sum of all of the stages determines the overall match winners.

The decision of the Match Director is final, based on the rulebook. If a rider wishes to protest the Match Director's decision he may do so upon filing a cash, $50, protest fee. Upon filing an appeal and paying the $50, an Appeals Board will be formed, consisting of three experienced riders who will hear the appeal. If the appeal is upheld, the riders score is adjusted as may be appropriate and the fee returned. If the appeal is denied, the protest fee is forfeited.

Each match should have an appeals board formed prior to the start of a match.

The board of a sponsoring club has sovereignty if no rule or penalty exists in the CMSA rulebook.

PENALTIES

Penalties should be avoided if at all possible. This can be accomplished through good

stage design and attention to detail. Procedural and discretionary penalties have no place in timed events and penalties should be restricted to the following.

Missed target: five seconds
Knocked over barrel: five seconds
Failure to follow course of fire: 10 seconds
Dropped gun: five seconds

A firearm that is dropped once the course has been engaged is a dead firearm and the rider incurs a five-second penalty plus any missed targets. A rider who drops a firearm, before crossing the (timing) beam, is removed from his place in line until the firearm has been cleaned and inspected by a match official. No consequences will be received for a firearm dropped after crossing the finish line, but the match official must still inspect the firearm.

If a rider falls from his horse or the horse trips and falls you may remount and continue your stage, it is your choice. If you feel you are unable to finish the stage then you will be given a time of 90 seconds. This includes any missed targets. You must be in control of your horse to engage any targets. The horse and rider must cross the timing beam together, but you do not have to be mounted.

If a rider fails to complete a course of fire on all stages, they should still be able to win the overall position or class if they are good enough to catch up to other contestants.

No penalty is to be given if a contestant knocks over a target pole, however the targets must be broken by direct gunfire with it being totally deflated prior to the rider leaving the arena. All targets whether standing or lying down must be broken to be considered a hit.

If a contestant hits two balloons with one shot he or she may use the remaining round to pick up a target he or she may have missed. If a round is not needed to pick up a missed target it should be fired before holstering or crossing the finish line.

A rider will have been determined to have engaged the course once he has crossed the start/finish line or is on the clock. Thereafter any mechanical malfunctions of your firearm or gear, including your horse, will not constitute a re-ride.

If a rider is notified during or after the completion of a stage that a timing malfunction occurred and no time was recorded, the rider will be granted a re-ride.

The match director will grant re-rides as soon as possible after the completion of that run. The rider must accept or decline his re-ride at this time. The score for that stage will be erased if the rider accepts or permanently entered if the re-ride is declined. Re-rides will normally take place after the last rider has completed the stage.

Re-rides are given as a new stage. This means he does not carry forward any misses nor a clean stage. (This is intended to make a rider decide whether he wants the re-ride and not wait to review the times of the other riders to decide if really needs to make up a re-ride)

If a run is interrupted a re-ride is a call made by the Range Master.

Misfires will be verified in the following manner: the suspect cartridge will be removed from the firearm and placed in the designated neutral gun as supplied by match officials and refired in the lateral position. This gun will be used to test all misfires for the entire match. Those rounds failing to fire will not be counted as a miss.

A jammed gun, due to a primer backing out or an otherwise faulty cartridge, will be verified by checking whether the primer pocket of such case was properly drilled out. If such a cartridge jammed the gun, a re-ride may be granted, as determined by the Match Director.

A squib shot shall be defined as a primer discharge whereby it is clear that the cartridge did not properly ignite and shall be ruled as an automatic hit on that target.

TARGETS

The standard targets used in CMSA competitions are helium quality balloons. When inflated, a target should measure six to nine inches in diameter. Care should be taken to make sure that targets are of uniform size for all competitors. Balloons of two distinctly different colors are recommended. It makes it easier for a contestant to define the first half from the second half of a stage.

For safety reasons target stands must be made of a flexible material like PVC or polyethylene pipe no larger than 3/4-inch in diameter. A simple 1-1/2-inch vertical hacksaw cut in the top of the pipe provides an excellent way to fasten the balloons to the target pole. Simply tie off the neck of the balloon, stretch it, slip it into the saw cut, then when let loose the balloon is securely fastened to the target pole.

Standard target poles should be 48-inches high. Traffic cones make excellent, safe bases for target poles.

SAFETY

All contestants are responsible for their own personal safety and that of their horse. They should also remain alert for other unsafe conditions and/or unsafe conduct by others. All contestants are considered safety officers and should take immediate action to remedy an unsafe condition or confront anyone whose conduct is unsafe.

SAFETY RULES AND GUIDELINES

- All firearms will be treated as if they are loaded.
- All loading and unloading of firearms should be done under the supervision of the designated armorer or safety officer.
- All firearms must remain unloaded until the rider is called to the loading area.
- All contestants must use the same "match-supplied" .45 Colt blank ammunition. Only one type of ammo will be used at a match. No personal ammunition of any type is to be allowed at CMSA competitions under penalty of disqualification. No blank should have an effective range longer than 20 feet for rider and spectator safety.
- No firearm should be cocked until immediately prior engaging a target.
- Competitors are expected to compete safely within their individual capabilities at all times. Do not try to "over ride" your own horsemanship skills. Control your firearm's muzzle direction at all times.
- All contestants must be knowledgeable and proficient in the safe use of firearms.
- Alcoholic beverages are prohibited in the range, staging and shooting areas. This includes all persons, competitors, range officials, guests, or anyone else in these areas.
- Competitors shall not consume any alcoholic beverage until they have completed all of their shooting for the day and have unloaded, inspected, and stored all of their firearms.
- Competitors will not ingest any substance, which may affect their ability to participate in a completely safe manner. Both prescription and non-prescription pharmaceuticals that may cause drowsiness or other physical or mental impairment are to be avoided.

- Contestants are to have no live ammunition on their person or in their cartridge belts or saddlebags. Dummy ammunition with inert or fired primers may be used in cartridge belts.

- Riders have final responsibility to make sure their firearms are loaded, check for missing or dented primers, cylinders rotate freely and to be certain they are properly indexed prior to stage engagement. The armorer is not responsible.

- Abusive language or conduct will not be tolerated and at discretion of Range Master may be given a warning or disqualification.

- Mandatory New Shooter orientation and qualification rides must be conducted PRIOR to competition.

- CMSA recommends the use of eye protection, ear protection and rubberbands on the feet, at all CMSA sanctioned matches.

IMPORTANT NOTICE

Cowboy mounted shooting requires equestrian and shooting skills of an intermediate to advanced level. Persons unsure as to their own skill level should contact the CMSA about qualifications, practice and pre-match training clinics.

CONTESTANT CLASSIFICATION

The CMSA has established a classification system that is based on the competitor's riding and shooting abilities. Like team roping and team penning, the CMSA has adopted a number classification system. Contestants are classified in five categories from one to five.

DIVISION ONE: A #1 class contestant is an entry-level rider. All new contestants until they win one buckle and move up or any current #2 who has not earned a #2 buckle can move down.

DIVISION TWO: Novice Rider/Shooter. A #2

class contestant has developed riding and shooting skills beyond that of a beginner. A #2 should be able to challenge a course of fire aggressively within the realm of his or her abilities. To move up to a Division #2, a competitor must earn one #1 buckle in a CMSA Point Qualifying Match. For a buckle/win to count there must be at least three #1 riders in the match.

DIVISION THREE: Accomplished Mounted Shooter. A #3 class contestant has a solid foundation in horsemanship and a proficiency with firearms. A #3 shooter is an experienced average shooter. To move up to a Division #3, a competi-

Like roping and team penning events, CMSA matches score contestants, not horses.

tor must earn two #2 buckles in a CMSA Point Qualifying Match. For a buckle/win to count there must be at least three #2 riders in match.

DIVISION FOUR: A Top Mounted Shooter. A #4 shooter is an experienced winning competitor possessing superb riding and shooting skills. A #4 contestant is an expert within the field. To move up to a Division #4, a competitor must earn three #3 buckles in a CMSA Point Qualifying Match. For a buckle/win to count there must be at least three #3 riders in match.

DIVISION FIVE: A Master Mounted Shooter. To move up to a Division #5, a competitor must earn five #4 buckles in a CMSA Point Qualifying Match or win a CMSA World or National Title to enter this Class. For a buckle/win to count there must be at least five #4 riders in match.

PEEWEE: Any Child 11 years old or under may join this class. Will only be allowed to move to Junior class when they turn 12 years old. PEEWEE's complete the course on horseback and shoot five rounds standing on the ground.

WOMEN'S DIVISION:

- Open Division: Any woman who is a CMSA #3, #4 or #5. Must move up in the same manner as men.
- Limited Division: Any woman who is a CMSA #1 or #2. Must move up in the same manner as men.

JUNIOR: Jr. Rider 16 and under. Juniors stay Juniors through their 16th calendar year. They have their own category and cannot place outside of it with the exception of Overall Champion, Reserve Champion or 3rd Overall.

- Open Division: Any junior who is a CMSA #3,

#4 or #5. Must move up in the same manner as men.
- Limited Division: Any junior who is a CMSA #1 or #2. Must move up in the same manner as men.

SENIOR CLASS: Any CMSA member, male or female, that is 55 or over may join this class. Contestant does not have to go into this category if he/she does not choose to.

CONTESTANT CLASSIFICATION CLARIFICATIONS

- When contestant reaches designated number of buckles in their current division they must move to the next division in their class.

- The word CHAMPION should be used for Overalls and Reserves only including Womens and Juniors. All others should be division WINNERS.

- Moving up in class will not be granted by verbal or written request. Movement will only be granted by number of wins in contestants existing class. #1's must win one #1 buckle, #2's must win two #2 buckles, #3's must win three #3 buckles, #4's must win five #4 buckles. For a win to qualify there must be at least three (3) other competitors in that class (except division #4 which must have five) and it must be a CMSA Point Qualifying Match.

- Moving down in class should be granted if a competitor has competed for one calendar year and not trophied in their current class.

- Anyone who wins a World or National title will become a #5 without moving up through the ranks.

TEAM EVENTS

The CMSA classification system forms the basis for team events. Teams are made up of three or fewer classified mounted contestants. A

#7, two-person team event is made up of two contestants whose total classification numbers total seven or fewer.

Examples:

A #4 and #3 equals a #7 team.

A #2 and #5 equals a #7 team.

Any team with total team number of seven or fewer is eligible for a #7 team. Team events can be scored concurrently with regular matches. Individual team member scores are totaled together to give team totals.

Teams can be made up of two or three members.

Two-member team: Total team number is seven.

Three-member team: Total team number is ten.

MISCELLANEOUS

Suggested event arena minimum size: 150 feet x 300 feet.

For Event Insurance call:
The Equestrian Group;
Amy Kelly (602) 992-1570

For information about Pegasus Timers;
Contact Randy Dumse at
New Micros (214) 339-2204

Event Trophies and Buckles:
Contact Frank Turben (602) 978-8328

CMSA supplies:
Frank Turben
4101 W. Willow
Phoenix, AZ 85029
(602) 978-8328
E-mail: turben@futureone.com

The CMSA recognizes only those events that are conducted under the rules and guidelines set forth in their handbook.

APPENDIX C

A RESOURCE LIST FOR COWBOY ACTION SHOOTERS

Alpha Tech Coatings, Inc.
32240 W. Bud Road
Maricopa, AZ 85239
(888) 974-3030
(602) 547-3034 (FAX)
www.aadam.com

American Arms, Incorporated
2607 NE Industrial Drive
North Kansas City, MO 64117
(816) 474-3161

American Derringer Corporation
127 North Lacy Drive
Waco, TX 76705
(817) 799-9111

Browning
One Browning Place
Morgan, UT 84050
(801) 876-2711

Buckaroo Bobbins
P.O. Box 1168
Chino Valley, AZ 86323
(catalog $2.00)

Cimarron Repeating Arms Company
P.O. Box 906
Fredericksburg, TX 78624-0906
(830) 997-9090

Colt's Manufacturing Company
P.O. Box 1868
Hartford, CT 06144
(800) 962-2658
www.colt.com

Cowboy Corral
219 N. Hwy 89A
Sedona, AZ 86336
(800) 457-2279

Cowboy Mounted Shooting Association (CMSA)
29317 N. 154th Place
Scottsdale, AZ 85262
www.cowboymountedshooting.com

Davis Industries
15150 Sierra Bonita Lane
Chino, CA 91710
(909) 597-4726
www.davisindguns.com

Dillon Precision Products, Inc.
8009 E. Dillon's Way
Scottsdale, AZ 85260
(480) 948-8009
(480) 998-2786 (FAX)
(800) 223-4570
www.dillonprecision.com

EMF Company, Incorporated
1900 East Warner Avenue, Suite 1-D
Santa Ana, CA 92705
(949) 261-6611

Goex, Incorporated
P.O. Box 659
Doyline, LA 71023
(318) 382-9300

Hodgdon Powder Company
P. O. Box 2932
Shawnee Mission, KS 66201
(913) 362-9455
www.hodgdon.com

H&R 1871, Incorporated
60 Industrial Rowe
Gardner, MA 01440
(978) 632-9393

Interarms
10 Prince Street
Alexandria, VA 22313
(703) 548-1400
www.interarms.com

James & Guns
7704 W. John Cabot
Glendale, AZ 85308
(602) 547-1942

Kicking Mule Outfitters
P.O. Box 836
Camp Verde, AZ 86322
(602) 567-2501

Lee's Gunsmithing
2777 Orange-Olive Road
Orange, CA 92665
(714) 921-9030

Lyman Products Corporation
475 Smith Street
Middletown, CT 06457
(860) 632-2020
www.lymanproducts.com

Marlin Firearms
100 Kenna Drive
North Haven, CT 06473
(203) 239-5621
www.marlin-guns.com

Munden Enterprises
1621 Sampson
Butte, MT 59701
(406) 494-2833
www.bob-munden.com

Navy Arms, Incorporated
689 Bergen Boulevard
Ridgefield, NJ 07657
(201) 945-2500
www.navyarms.com

Oglesby & Oglesby Gunmakers, Incorporated
744 W. Andrew Rd.
Springfield, IL 62707
(217) 487-7100

Olathe Boot Company
705 South Kansas
Olathe, KS 66061
(913) 764-5110 (In Kansas)
(800) 255-6126 (Outside Kansas)

Peacemaker Specialists
P.O. Box 157
Whitmore, CA 96096
(916) 472-3438 (catalog $1.00)

River Junction Trade Company
No 312 Main Street
McGregor, IA 52157
(319) 873-2387 (catalog $5.00)

Rossi S. A.
16175 NW 49th Avenue
Miami, FL 33014
(305) 474-0401

Scully/Wah-Maker
1701 Pacific Avenue
Oxnard, CA
(805) 483-6339
www.wahmaker.com

Shiloh Rifle Manufacturing
Box 279
Big Timber, MT 59011
(406) 932-4454

Single Action Shooting Society (S.A.S.S.)
1938 North Batavia Street, Suite C
Orange, CA 92665
(714) 998-1899 (Send $2 for information)
www.sassnet.com

Stetson Hats
601 Marion Drive
Garland, TX 75042
(800) 325-2662

Stewart Saddlery
PO Box 1328
Ft. Gibson, OK 74434
(520) 537-7077 (catalog $3.00)

Stoeger Industries
5 Mansard Court
Wayne, NJ 07470
(201) 440-2700

Sturm, Ruger & Company, Incorporated
200 Ruger Rd.
Prescott, AZ 86301
www.ruger-firearms.com

Tonto Rim Trading Co.
5028 N. Hwy 31
Seymour, IN 47274
(800) 242-4287

Uberti-USA, Inc.
P.O. Box 509
Lakeville, CT 06039
(203) 435-8068

United States Firearms Manufacturing Company
55 Van Dyke Ave
Hartford, CT 06106
(860) 724-1152
www.usfirearms.com

White's Handmade Boots
Spokane, WA
800-541-3786

Wild West Mercantile
5130 N 19th Avenue, Suite 6
Phoenix, AZ 85015
(800) 596-0444
(602) 246-6078 (catalog $3.00)
www.wwmerc.com

Winchester/U.S. Repeating Arms Company, Inc.
275 Winchester Avenue
Morgan, UT 84050-9333
(801) 876-3440
www.winchester-guns.com

N ow repeat after me: "The Cowboy must never shoot first, hit a smaller man, or take unfair advantage…."

GENE AUTRY

Gene Autry started his career in 1928 on radio as a singer. By the time of his retirement in the early 1960s, Gene had successfully transitioned from radio to motion pictures and television. His "B" Western movies were decidedly modern, and included automobiles, radios and airplanes, as well as sixguns and guitars. He had his own television series, and wrote over 200 songs. After retiring as a performer, Gene went on to become owner of the California Angels baseball team (now the Anaheim Angels) and to found the Gene Autry Museum of Western Heritage.

Gene Autry's Cowboy Code

1. The Cowboy must never shoot first, hit a smaller man, or take unfair advantage.
2. He must never go back on his word, or a trust confided in him.
3. He must always tell the truth.
4. He must be gentle with children, the elderly, and animals.
5. He must not advocate or possess racially or religiously intolerant ideas.
6. He must help people in distress.
7. He must be a good worker
8. He must keep himself clean in thought, speech, action, and personal habits.
9. He must respect women, parents, and his nation's laws.
10. The Cowboy is a patriot.

Orvon Gene Autry
September 29, 1907 – October 2, 1998

JOHN WAYNE
THE DUKE

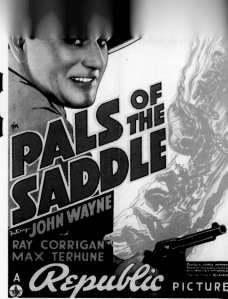

Where do you start with an actor like John Wayne? "The Duke" actually transcended the roles he played as an actor to assume the status of cultural icon. He BECAME America in the eyes of several generations of young boys, if not in the eyes of the world. Yet, the icon's start in Hollywood was a humble one. In exchange for USC football tickets, cowboy star Tom Mix got young Marion Morrison a summer job as a prop man. This job led to a friendship with director John Ford who began casting him in bit parts, in some of which he was billed as "John Wayne." He paid his dues in more than 80 B movies before John Ford cast him in the lead role in "Stagecoach" in 1939. Nominated for Best Actor for his performance in "Sands of Iwo Jima," he finally won the Oscar for a western role: as Rooster Cogburn in "True Grit." True to his "B" Western roots, The Duke took the cowboy role to heart, and elevated the status of the western movie

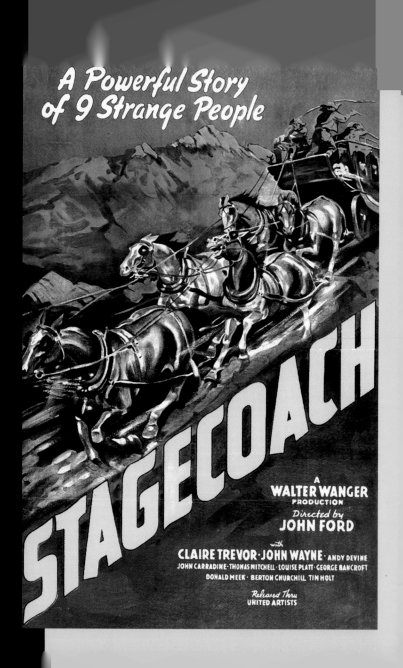